Here's all the great literature in this grade level of *Celebrate Reading!*

"Mom, Mom, My Ears Are Growing!"

And Other Joys of the Real World

Bingo Brown, Gypsy Lover
from the novel by
Betsy Byars
✹ *School Library Journal* Best Book
✹ ALA Notable Children's Book

The Cybil War
from the novel by
Betsy Byars
✹ ALA Notable Children's Book
✹ Children's Choice

Remarkable Children
from the book by
Dennis Brindell Fradin

And Still I Rise
from the collection by
Maya Angelou
✹ *School Library Journal* Best Book

How It Feels to Fight for Your Life
from the book by
Jill Krementz
✹ Outstanding Science Trade Book
✹ Teachers' Choice

Fast Sam, Cool Clyde, and Stuff
from the novel by
Walter Dean Myers
✹ Children's Choice

The Summer of the Falcon
from the novel by
Jean Craighead George
✹ Newbery Medal Author

Featured Poet
Maya Angelou

Look Both Ways
Seeing the Other Side

Free to Fly

A User's Guide to the Imagination

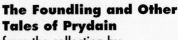

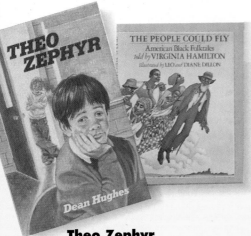

Theo Zephyr
from the novel by
Dean Hughes
✳ Children's Choice

The People Could Fly:
American Black Folktales
from the collection by
Virginia Hamilton
Illustrations by Leo and
Diane Dillon
✳ *New York Times* Best Illustrated
✳ ALA Notable Children's Book

Joyful Noise: Poems
for Two Voices
from the collection by
Paul Fleischman
✳ Newbery Medal

The Town Cat and
Other Tales
from the collection by
Lloyd Alexander
✳ Newbery Medal Author
✳ American Book
   Award Author

The Foundling and Other
Tales of Prydain
from the collection by
Lloyd Alexander
✳ *School Library Journal*
   Best Book

Cinderella Finds Time
by Val R. Cheatham

In Search of Cinderella
by Shel Silverstein
✳ ALA Notable Children's Book

Glass Slipper
by Jane Yolen
✳ Kerlan Award Author

...And Then the Prince
Knelt Down and Tried
to Put the Glass Slipper
on Cinderella's Foot
by Judith Viorst
✳ Christopher Award Author

Yeh Shen: A Cinderella Story
from China
retold by Ai-Ling Louie
Illustrations by Ed Young
✳ ALA Notable Children's Book

Featured Poets
Paul Fleischman
Pat Mora
Shel Silverstein
Jane Yolen
Judith Viorst

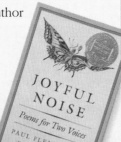

Journey Home
and Other Routes to Belonging

Featured Poets
Gwendolyn Brooks
Edwin Muir

Arriving Before I Start
Passages Through Time

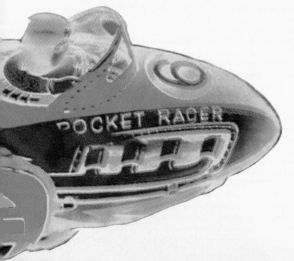

Just Like a Hero
Talk About Leadership

The Revenge of the Incredible Dr. Rancid and His Youthful Assistant, Jeffrey
from the novel by
Ellen Conford
✳ Young Readers' Choice
Award Author

The Gold Coin
by Alma Flor Ada
✳ Christopher Award

Mother Teresa
from the biography by
Patricia Reilly Giff

Prince of the Double Axe
by Madeleine Polland

Featured Poet
John Greenleaf Whittier

Celebrate Reading!
Trade Book Library

**Our Sixth-Grade
Sugar Babies**
by Eve Bunting
✳ *School Library Journal* Best Book

Goodbye, Chicken Little
by Betsy Byars
✳ Children's Choice
✳ Children's Editors' Choice
✳ Library of Congress
Children's Book
✳ *New York Times* Notable Book

Dragon of the Lost Sea
by Laurence Yep
✳ ALA Notable Children's Book
✳ International Reading Association
100 Favorite Paperbacks of 1989

The Westing Game
by Ellen Raskin
✳ Newbery Medal
✳ Boston Globe-Horn Book Award

**The Brocaded Slipper and
Other Vietnamese Tales**
by Lynette Vuong

The Jedera Adventure
by Lloyd Alexander
✳ Parents' Choice

**The Endless Steppe:
Growing Up in Siberia**
by Esther Hautzig
✳ ALA Notable Children's Book
✳ Boston Globe-Horn Book Award
Honor Book
✳ Lewis Carroll Shelf Award

**Baseball in April
and Other Stories**
by Gary Soto
✳ ALA Notable Children's Book
✳ *Parenting* Reading-Magic Award

Tom's Midnight Garden
by Philippa Pearce
✳ Carnegie Medal Winner

The House of Dies Drear
by Virginia Hamilton
✳ ALA Notable Children's Book

**Journey to Jo'burg:
A South African Story**
by Beverly Naidoo
✳ Notable Social Studies Trade Book

Jackie Joyner-Kersee
by Neil Cohen

Free to Fly

A USER'S GUIDE TO THE IMAGINATION

Titles in This Set

About the Cover Artist

Lisa Desimini started drawing when she was ten years old, drawing
on flattened cardboard boxes because she could get them free. In
high school she painted elaborate designs on her friends' denim
jackets. Today she illustrates many books and book covers.

ISBN: 0-673-81168-9

1997
Scott, Foresman and Company, Glenview, Illinois
All Rights Reserved.
Printed in the United States of America.

Acknowledgments appear on page 136.

2345678910DQ010099989796

Free to Fly

A USER'S GUIDE TO THE IMAGINATION

ScottForesman

A Division of HarperCollins*Publishers*

CONTENTS

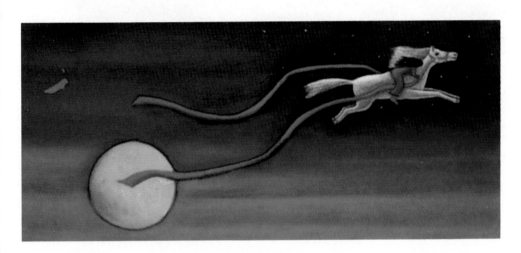

Imaginations

Lloyd Alexander's Creations
Author Study

Interpretations
Genre Study

Student Resources

Just call me Theo

by Dean Hughes

When the door opened, all the kids looked up. They were supposed to be doing their math assignment, but it was Monday, and any interruption was welcome.

What they saw, however, was something no one could have expected. It was a boy—a strange one— and he was just standing there, grinning. He was short and round-faced, with chubby cheeks. His ears were big, and they stuck out through some loose, rather ragged-looking hair. He was wearing baggy green pants and an old brown shirt that was too big for him. His grin looked silly, his teeth too big for his mouth, and yet, there was something appealing about him, like a dog you like because he's sort of ugly.

All the kids in the class were surprised, but Brad Hill was almost knocked off his chair. He blinked and shook his head the way characters in a cartoon movie do, and then he whispered to himself, "It couldn't be him." But it was. The clothes were different, but that was all. Brad knew that face too well to be mistaken.

Mrs. Hardy said, "May I help you?" She was sitting at her desk on the opposite side of the room.

"Yes, ma'am," the boy said. His voice was surprising—deep and clean, like a radio announcer's. He walked across the front of the room, taking long strides with his short legs, and he stopped near Mrs. Hardy and put his hand out. The other hand was stuck deep in his pants pocket. "I'm Theo," he said. "I assume you are Mrs. Hardy. I'm most happy to meet you—and honored to be one of your sixth-grade students."

That's not his name, Brad thought. *And his voice sounds different. Maybe he's just some kid who looks a lot like . . . but that's his face. I know it is.*

Mrs. Hardy took hold of the boy's hand and gave it a little shake, but she seemed rather mystified. "You're in my class?" she said.

"Yes, ma'am. I've only just arrived in Grandview." The way he said it was strange, as though he meant "just this very minute."

Mrs. Hardy was a person who always knew what to do in any situation, but she acted a little confused right now. The kid didn't let that bother him. He turned toward the class and said, "Allow me to introduce myself. I'm Theo Zephyr. That's spelled Z-E-P-H-Y-R. Zeh-fer. But just call me Theo. Now if you'll each tell me your own name, I promise never to forget."

"Just a moment," Mrs. Hardy said, standing up. "I really think . . . Perhaps it would be better if . . ."

Mrs. Hardy was staring. She always told the kids not to stare, but she was doing it herself. And so were all the students, except the ones who were ducking their heads, trying not to laugh. Brad was still blinking. There was no way this could be happening; he really wondered whether he was having some kind of weird hallucination.

"Oh, excuse me, ma'am," Theo said. "I didn't mean to come in and start taking over. I'm afraid I have a tendency to do that. You just tell me when I get out of line."

Mrs. Hardy nodded but said nothing for a moment. She was a gentle woman, pretty, with a nice smile, but she knew how to be firm when she had to be. That's why it was so strange to see her this rattled. "Why don't we step out into the hall for just a moment?" she finally said. "I need to…find out more about you."

"Oh, excellent," Theo said. "Wonderful idea. I can always learn the children's names later."

A number of kids started to laugh, but Mrs. Hardy gave them a serious look and then said, "Well, actually, it's fine if you want to learn their names. Students, why don't you each say your name. Cynthia, would you like to start?"

The kids began to announce their names, and Theo listened carefully, sometimes asking to hear one a second time or asking for the spelling. Brad hesitated for just a moment when his turn came, and Theo said, with a big grin, "I know Brad. Brad Hill. I've known him for years and years."

Brad gave his head a quick shake. *Don't do this,* he wanted to shout. But Theo looked to the next person in the row. Brad took a deep breath of relief and looked down, his dark hair falling over his eyebrows. He touched his desk to see if it felt . . . normal. If this was a dream, could everything seem so real?

When all the students had given their names, Mrs. Hardy stepped toward the door, but Theo looked over to the first seat and said, "All right. Cynthia Bauer, Philip Matheson, Carl Zavala, Nancy Price, Steve Bascom, Kerstin Hansen, Jennifer Keith, Jeff Le Duc. . . ." And so he continued all the way around the room. He really didn't seem to be showing off, but he got every name exactly right. Then he turned and said, "Now, Mrs. Hardy, should we have that little chat?"

Not a whole lot of math was done while Mrs. Hardy and Theo were gone. Everyone was whispering back and forth, saying how weird this Theo guy was. But they seemed excited, as though they thought he was going to add a little life to the place.

What if he tells them? Brad was thinking. *Or what if they figure it out? I'd have to move somewhere else. I'd have to run away from home. But it couldn't be him. Things like that don't happen.*

"How do you know that kid?"

Brad looked up. Gil Brimhall was in the next row and a couple of seats ahead, but he was twisting around in his seat. Brad didn't want Gil, of all people, to know. "I don't know him," Brad said. "He must have me mixed up with someone else."

"He knew your name."

Brad tried to think of some explanation. And then he said weakly, "I don't know how he knew me. Maybe he used to live in my neighborhood or something."

"Don't you remember him?"

"No."

"Man, I don't see how you could forget him." And then he added sarcastically, "You two should hit it off. You're about the same size."

Brad was actually bigger—quite a bit bigger—but he didn't say that. He just let it go. Gil thought of himself as such a hotshot; he *would* be the one to start asking questions.

When Mrs. Hardy came back, Theo was right behind her. He commented softly that he liked the way she had decorated the room. "I like daffodils," he said, with that dumb grin still on his face. Brad couldn't believe it. Why was he doing stuff like that? But once Theo sat down at a desk, behind Brad and to the right, he settled in and didn't say a word until recess. Brad looked back at him once, and Theo smiled and waved. After that, Brad didn't look again.

At recess all the kids were eager to find out more about Theo. Several of them crowded around him and started asking questions. He was happy to talk to them, but Mrs. Hardy came along and said, "If you're going to play softball, you'd better get started. Why don't you keep the same teams as last week so you won't have to choose again?"

It had been a cold spring in Utah, and the kids had only been able to play softball for the last few days, even though it was getting to be late in April.

Everyone seemed to agree to keep the same teams, but Gil Brimhall turned to Alan Cuell and said, "You guys have to take that goofy new kid."

"No way," Alan said. "We've already got Merrill on our team, and Betsy—neither one can—"

"Boys, that's enough," Mrs. Hardy said. "Maybe we *should* choose over again if you're—"

"No, that's okay. We'll take him," Gil said, but he obviously wasn't pleased.

As the kids walked onto the field, Theo waited, as though he wasn't sure what he should do. Gil finally yelled over to him, "So what position do you usually play?"

"I'm trying to think. The only time he had me play, I think it was something called central field."

Brad was not far away. He froze. But Gil didn't ask who "he" was. He just said, "It's called *center.* Are you telling me you've only played one time?"

"Well, no. Many times. But it was always the same plays over and over. Except batting. Sometimes I played batter. Isn't that what it's called when you hit the ball?"

Gil was staring. It's hard to say what he might have said if Mrs. Hardy hadn't stepped in. "Gil, that will be fine. Just let him play center field."

"Thank you, Mrs. Hardy," Theo said, even though Gil had said nothing to agree. "I know where that is." Out Theo trotted, his baggy pants and shirt billowing in the breeze as he ran.

Brad waited his turn at bat, standing a little away from the others. He thought maybe he knew what was going on now. And then, when the first batter hit a high fly to short center, he was sure of it.

Theo came loping in a little way and stood under the ball. He made a nice catch with his bare hands. Gil, who had been playing shortstop, had tried to get to the ball, so he was not far away when Theo caught it.

He stopped suddenly and took a long look, as though he had just witnessed a miracle. Theo grinned with those big teeth and then tossed the ball to Gil. "That's called an 'out.' Right?"

"Yeah. Way to go."

It was happening. Just the way it always did. But it couldn't be. Brad felt his eyelids to see if they really were open.

They were, and the next play was just the one he expected. The batter was Richard Bills, a small kid like Brad. Gil yelled out in a booming voice, "Move up. Richard can't hit." Gil himself moved in very tight, not all that far from the pitcher. Richard swung a couple of times and missed, and gradually Gil worked in even closer. But on the next pitch Richard hit the ball fairly hard, and it got past Gil before he could react. He stomped his foot in disgust, and then he turned around to see where the ball had ended up.

But there was Theo, about where the shortstop would normally play. He had already scooped the ball up and was firing it to first. Richard was out by a mile.

Theo nodded to Gil and grinned. With those big ears and that crazy hair, he looked like a kid who could never do anything right. But he had just made the best play any of the kids had ever seen, and all he did was turn and trot back to "central" field. Gil spun around and looked at Phil Matheson, who was pitching. "How did he do that?"

"He ran. Didn't you see him?"

"No. I was turned the other way."

"He's the fastest kid in the world. He's got to be."

He'd better not keep this up, Brad was thinking. *They're going to figure out what's going on.* In spite of Brad's nervousness, however, he was getting some

pleasure too. It was nice to see someone show up Gil. When all this had happened in Brad's mind for the first time, it was just a wish, a daydream like the many daydreams Brad immersed himself in, but seeing it for real like this was a little too good.

The next batter was stepping up. It was Terry Burningham, one of the best hitters. He let a couple of pitches go by, and then he really slugged one. The left fielder took off after it, but he had no chance of catching up. And then Theo came shooting out of nowhere. He was really motoring, those little legs just a blur. The ball seemed to hang in space as Theo closed in on it; then he turned—just the way the major leaguers do—and reached out and caught it with one hand.

Terry had already rounded first base, and he kept running to second, as though he still couldn't accept what had just happened. Gil looked out to left field for a while, and then he turned back and looked at Phil. His eyes were the size of softballs. Theo, meanwhile, was galloping toward the infield, his wild hair blowing straight back. He was waving the ball over his head.

"We get to bat now, I believe," he said as he approached.

"How did you do that?" Gil said.

"Do what?"

"Run so fast. I've never seen a kid who could run that fast."

"Really?" Theo looked curious, as though he had never thought of such a thing. He looked over at Brad, who was hurrying toward him.

Brad grabbed Theo's shoulder and spun him away from Gil. "Don't do the rest," he whispered.

"Why not? That's how it always ends. I hit—"

"Shut up. Keep your voice down. What are you doing here anyway?"

"What I always do. I don't see what you're getting so upset about."

But Gil was yelling. "Come on, Theo. You're going to lead off. We want to see if you can hit too."

Brad was doomed. He walked out to right field. This next one was going to push things too far. No one was going to believe it. Whatever satisfaction he had found in seeing Gil look so amazed was going to be lost if . . .

Sure enough, Theo hit the first pitch out of sight—over the fence, over the street, over the hill, and all the way down into the park below. Nobody could do that. Brad watched the ball sail away, and then he looked back to see what the kids were going to say. But they weren't saying anything. They were staring off at the sky as though they had just witnessed a UFO. Half a minute went by, and no one even moved.

Then Theo said, "Do I run around the bases now?"

Gil looked at him strangely, as though he had been brought back to reality a little too suddenly. "If you want to," he finally said. And so little Theo went zipping around the bases, not putting out much effort but *really* traveling.

When he got back, all the kids were still just standing there, most of them looking at Theo now. The kids in the field had begun to walk toward home plate. Brad, however, was taking his time. Mrs. Hardy eventually said, distantly, "I suppose we'll never find the ball."

"Oh, I'm sorry. I'll retrieve it," Theo said, and he was off again. He glided out to the big chainlink fence, and he scrambled up and dropped down on the other side as if it was something he did all the time, and then he charged across the street and over the hill.

"I'm getting that kid for my summer-league team," Gil said reverently.

"Yeah, if the major leagues don't get him first," someone said.

Then Theo reappeared and ran back across the street. He stopped just beyond the fence and threw the ball all the way to home plate, on the fly. No one even tried to catch it. They watched it bounce away, and then they all looked around at each other. Paulette Chambers said, softly, "No one can throw a ball that far."

Brad felt a chill go through him. How long before the kids figured out what was going on?

The rest of the day Theo was hardly noticeable. He seemed very busy with his studies. The other students remained in a state of shock. All day they kept twisting around to look back at Theo, as though they wanted to verify that he really existed. Mrs. Hardy seemed also to be trying to convince herself that everything really was normal, that what she had seen could somehow be explained. "Well," she said at one point, "our new student certainly is a wonderful athlete. We've learned that much about him."

"Thank you, Mrs. Hardy," Theo said, in that big voice of his. "And you're a wonderful teacher. I've enjoyed this day immensely."

Kids weren't even laughing anymore. They all turned around and got another look. What kind of kid was this?

At the end of the day, Brad got to Theo quickly and kept him at the back of the class while everyone else was leaving. "Look," he whispered, "I don't know what you're trying to do, but you've got to get out of here."

"Leave? Already? I've only done one of your daydreams so far."

"That stuff isn't real. It can't happen in the real world. They'll all figure that out pretty soon."

"Real world? You mean there's more than one world?" Theo seemed quite amazed to hear such a thing.

Brad was without words. Where did he even start? What could you say to someone like this?

Gil had stayed around, and now he came up behind Brad and said, "Hey, Theo, I want to talk to you."

"Oh, how nice," Theo said. "I'm hoping to be your friend, if I can. I've seen you lots of times, but I just don't feel I know you very well."

"Seen me? Where?"

Brad spoke quickly. "He just told me he used to live around here. He's watched us play ball and some stuff like that."

"Yes, I suppose that's a way of thinking of it," Theo said thoughtfully, "except that—"

"We'd better get out of here," Brad said. "Mrs. Hardy probably wants to leave."

That was not true. Mrs. Hardy was at her desk, busy with some sort of paperwork. But she took this chance to say, "Theo, could I speak to you for a moment?"

"Certainly. Certainly." He strode to her desk. Brad and Gil waited, and Brad could hear what Mrs. Hardy said, even though she kept her voice down.

"This has been a very strange day, Theo. You sort of took me by surprise. When you came in, I naturally assumed you had been admitted by the principal, and that your parents had come in—all the usual things. But I talked to Dr. Buchmiller this afternoon, and he said he had never heard of you. He didn't get your records or—"

"Tell me about records and I'll see that he gets some."

"Well, you know, the school you came from, birth certificate, proof of residency, test scores—all the things in your file."

"Don't you think I can handle sixth grade?"

"Oh, it's not that at all. It's just the way things are

done. You have to come over with your parents and sign in officially. It's not enough just to move into town and show up at a class."

"Ah, I see. I never quite comprehend the way people think about such things. All right. By tomorrow Dr. Buchmiller will say everything is okay."

"Well, fine. But you know he might not assign you to my class. There are two other sixth-grade classes."

"Oh, I see. Well, I'll take care of that too."

"Take care of it? Theo, you can't do that. He's the one who will have to make the decision."

Theo reached out and put his hand on Mrs. Hardy's shoulder. "I like you, Mrs. Hardy," he said. "You'll get used to me. You'll get so you don't mind the way I am."

"I don't . . . mind . . . exactly."

"I'll see you tomorrow." He turned, or rather, spun in place, and took ten giant steps to the door. "Come on, Gil," he said, "let's have that talk."

When the boys got outside, Gil said, "Theo, how would you like to be an Arctic Circle Tiger this summer?"

Theo stopped and turned toward Gil. He looked shocked. "Oh, no. I do people. I don't want to be a tiger."

"What?"

"I don't know how to think like a tiger. I can't picture myself going around like that, on all fours."

"What?"

"Do they even *have* tigers in the Arctic Circle?"

"What are you talking about?"

"No, no, Theo," Brad said. "He means a baseball team. They're called the Tigers. They're sponsored by the Arctic Circle—it's a fast-food place." Then Brad

stepped closer and gave Theo a firm look of warning before he turned to Gil. "But Theo told me he's not staying around here very long. He won't be here this summer. In fact, he might be gone really soon."

"How come?" Gil asked, looking at Theo, not at Brad. "Didn't you just move here?"

"Well, it depends on how you think about it. I guess I don't use words quite the same way you do. 'Move,' to me, means—"

"His parents are just thinking about moving here. They might not stay. In fact, it doesn't look like they will."

Some of the other boys in their class had walked over in time to hear what Brad had said. Phil asked, "Where did you used to live?"

Theo thought about that, and Brad held his breath. If Theo said just the wrong thing, and everyone figured out what was going on, Brad was going to look like an idiot.

"I'm never very clear about that," Theo finally said. "I suppose you mean 'what place?' Like a city or a town or a country. To me—"

"California," Brad said. "He lived in California most of his—"

"Only on those vacations," Theo said. "Two years ago when you went to Disneyland, and—"

"Let's play some basketball," Brad said. He was in a panic. "Come on. Let's shoot some hoops."

Apparently the other guys had just been heading to do that. Phil had a basketball under his arm.

"Oh, yes. I like that one," Theo said. "Let's do the one where we play basketball. Gil, you're in it."

"What?"

"Wait a minute," Brad said, and he grabbed hold of Theo and started pulling him away. "Just a second. I've got to talk to Theo."

"Brad, please," Theo was saying. "That's really quite impolite."

But Brad was whispering, "What the heck do you think you're doing?"

"The basketball one on the playground. I can't do the one with the crowd right away. That will take some arrangements."

"Don't do any of them. Get out of here. Just go away now and don't come back."

"But I thought you wanted me to do all this stuff."

"Not out loud. Or, I mean . . . not out where people can watch."

"Brad, I don't know what you're talking about. I don't mean to sound rude, but you really don't make any sense sometimes." Theo walked away, over to the other boys. "Okay, let's form the teams. Gil guards me."

The boys glanced around at each other, obviously baffled, but then they formed two teams of three. Brad was on the team with Theo, since he was also small. By now, they knew enough to expect big things from Theo. All the tall guys—Gil, Phil, and Brian Jorgensen—were on the other team.

What followed was an incredible dribbling and shooting exhibition. It was a one-man show that would put any player on the Globetrotters to shame. At first Theo would fake Gil in the air, dribble past him, and hit the easy lay-up. But pretty soon all three guys were guarding Theo, so he started dribbling between his legs, behind his back, in and out, around and through those guys, and then popping in jump shots from all over the place. He could jump so high he could even out-rebound them when they missed shots.

On defense, he would steal the ball right out of their hands, or if the guys stayed back and tried to shoot from outside, he would block their shots. After about four minutes the score was sixteen to nothing. Brad called time-out. The guys on the other team were standing there huffing and puffing and looking at each other in wonderment. Alan Cuell was just as amazed. He was on Theo's team but had never touched the ball. After the first couple of plays he had just stood there and watched.

"He's pretty good, isn't he?" Brad said and tried to laugh; then he said, "Come here, Theo."

Theo marched away from the others. "Did you see Gil's face?" he asked. "That's what you love—that stunned look on his face. I'll do the big finish on him. That's your favorite."

"Theo, listen to me. No one can play basketball like that. They know that. They're not stupid. If you keep this up, they're going to catch on. If they figure out that I thought all this stuff up, they'll —"

"But I always play basketball like that. I do those same plays every time. Just in different order."

"I know that. But it's just made up. You can't . . . really . . ." Brad let his breath blow out. This was crazy. He was dreaming. He knew he was. He gave his head a quick knock—but it hurt. "Things like this don't happen, Theo."

"I didn't think you would call me by that name."

"Hey, that's the only thing you've done right so far. If you had used your real name, they would have caught on already."

"You use words in the oddest ways, Brad. You keep changing what 'real' means. Now, come on. I'll do the big finish. You've always loved it before."

There was nothing to say. This wasn't really happening anyway. Brad decided just to follow along and get this over with; then he was going to have to figure out a way to wake up.

Theo took the ball and dribbled steadily, standing in one place. He waited for Gil to come out to cover. Gil was looking determined, unwilling to let this little guy beat him again. Theo dribbled to his right, slowly, allowing Gil to stay close, and then suddenly he did a quick pivot and a behind-the-back dribble, and drove past Gil on the left. Gil was still standing there like a statue. When he finally reacted and spun around, he was just in time to see Theo fly through the air, rotate one hundred eighty degrees, and do a behind-the-head, two-hand slam dunk.

Gil just stood there staring for quite some time, and then he said, in a voice that was now angry, "You can't do that." Brad didn't know whether to laugh or cry, but he had to admit, it was nice seeing Gil this frustrated.

"I just did," Theo said and smiled in that friendly way of his.

"You're too short."

Theo looked over at Brad. "He's saying strange things too. He's supposed to say—"

Brad dashed to Theo and grabbed him again. "You come with me right now," he whispered, and then, louder, "Well, we'll see you guys later." He was pushing Theo, with his hand in the middle of his back. The two of them were well down the block before Brad dared to look around. All four guys were still standing where they had been. But they were not talking; they were looking up at the basket, as though they were trying to decide whether they had seen what they had seen.

"I think they're on to us," Brad said. "You're talking too much."

But when Brad looked back to Theo, he received the biggest jolt of the day—and he had already had some beauties. Theo was gone. He had simply vanished.

Thinking About It

1. You are in Mrs. Hardy's class the day Theo arrives. What do you think of Theo? When do you figure out that Theo is very, very different from the other students?

2. Is Theo a typical imaginary friend? How is Theo different from most people's fantasy friends? Is he a real threat to Brad? Be Brad and tell your innermost thoughts about Theo.

3. Invite your daydream friend into your class. What is your daydream friend's name? What extraordinary powers does your fantasy friend possess? What happens?

Another Book by Dean Hughes

In *Nutty and the Case of the Ski-Slope Spy,* Nutty Nutsell and his friends take a ski trip to Utah and find mystery and adventure on the slopes.

The People

Told by VIRGINIA HAMILTON

FLY

Could

They say the people could fly. Say that long ago in Africa, some of the people knew magic. And they would walk up on the air like climbin up on a gate. And they flew like blackbirds over the fields. Black, shiny wings flappin against the blue up there.

Then, many of the people were captured for Slavery. The ones that could fly shed their wings. They couldn't take their wings across the water on the slave ships. Too crowded, don't you know.

The folks were full of misery, then. Got sick with the up and down of the sea. So they forgot about flyin when they could no longer breathe the sweet scent of Africa.

Say the people who could fly kept their power, although they shed their wings. They kept their secret magic in the land of slavery. They looked the same as the other people from Africa who had been coming over, who had dark skin. Say you couldn't tell anymore one who could fly from one who couldn't.

One such who could was an old man, call him Toby. And standin tall, yet afraid, was a young woman who once had wings. Call her Sarah. Now Sarah carried a babe tied to her back. She trembled to be so hard worked and scorned.

The slaves labored in the fields from sunup to sundown. The owner of the slaves callin himself their Master. Say he was a hard lump of clay. A hard, glinty coal. A hard rock pile, wouldn't be moved. His Overseer on horseback pointed out the slaves who were slowin down. So the one called Driver cracked his whip over the slow ones to make them move faster. That whip was a slice-open cut of pain. So they did move faster. Had to.

Sarah hoed and chopped the row as the babe on her back slept.

Say the child grew hungry. That babe started up bawling too loud. Sarah couldn't stop to feed it. Couldn't stop to soothe and quiet it down. She let it cry. She didn't want to. She had no heart to croon to it.

"Keep that thing quiet," called the Overseer. He pointed his finger at the babe. The woman scrunched low. The Driver cracked his whip across the babe anyhow. The babe hollered like any hurt child, and the woman fell to the earth.

The old man that was there, Toby, came and helped her to her feet.

"I must go soon," she told him.

"Soon," he said.

Sarah couldn't stand up straight any longer. She was too weak. The sun burned her face. The babe cried and cried, "Pity me, oh, pity me," say it sounded like. Sarah was so sad and starvin, she sat down in the row.

"Get up, you black cow," called the Overseer. He pointed his hand, and the Driver's whip snarled around Sarah's legs. Her sack dress tore into rags. Her legs bled onto the earth. She couldn't get up.

Toby was there where there was no one to help her and the babe.

"Now, before it's too late," panted Sarah. "Now, Father!"

"Yes, Daughter, the time is come," Toby answered. "Go, as you know how to go!"

He raised his arms, holding them out to her. *"Kum . . . yali, kum buba tambe,"* and more magic words, said so quickly, they sounded like whispers and sighs.

The young woman lifted one foot on the air. Then the other. She flew clumsily at first, with the child now held tightly in her arms. Then she felt the magic, the African mystery. Say she rose just as free as a bird. As light as a feather.

The Overseer rode after her, hollerin. Sarah flew over the fences. She flew over the woods. Tall trees could not snag her. Nor could the Overseer. She flew like an eagle

now, until she was gone from sight. No one dared speak about it. Couldn't believe it. But it was, because they that was there saw that it was.

Say the next day was dead hot in the fields. A young man slave fell from the heat. The Driver come and whipped him. Toby come over and spoke words to the fallen one. The words of ancient Africa once heard are never remembered completely. The young man forgot them as soon as he heard them. They went way inside him. He got up and rolled over on the air. He rode it awhile. And he flew away.

Another and another fell from the heat. Toby was there. He cried out to the fallen and reached his arms out to them. *"Kum kunka yali, kum . . . tambe!"* Whispers and sighs. And they too rose on the air. They rode the hot breezes. The ones flyin were black and shinin sticks, wheelin above the head of the Overseer. They crossed the rows, the fields, the fences, the streams, and were away.

"Seize the old man!" cried the Overseer. "I heard him say the magic *words*. Seize him!"

The one callin himself Master come runnin. The Driver got his whip ready to curl around old Toby and tie him up. The slaveowner took his hip gun from its place. He meant to kill old, black Toby.

But Toby just laughed. Say he threw back his head and said, "Hee, hee! Don't you know who I am? Don't you know some of us in this field?" He said it to their faces. "We are ones who fly!"

And he sighed the ancient words that were a dark promise. He said them all around to the others in the field under the whip, ". . . *buba yali . . . buba tambe. . . .*"

There was a great outcryin. The bent backs straighted up. Old and young who were called slaves and could fly joined hands. Say like they would ring-sing. But they didn't shuffle in a circle. They didn't sing. They rose on the air. They flew in a flock that was black against the heavenly blue. Black crows or black shadows. It didn't matter, they went so high. Way above the plantation, way over the slavery land. Say they flew away to *Free-dom*.

And the old man, old Toby, flew behind them, takin care of them. He wasn't cryin. He wasn't laughin. He was the seer. His gaze fell on the plantation where the slaves who could not fly waited.

"Take us with you!" Their looks spoke it but they were afraid to shout it. Toby couldn't take them with him.

Hadn't the time to teach them to fly. They must wait for a chance to run.

"Goodie-bye!" The old man called Toby spoke to them, poor souls! And he was flyin gone.

So they say. The Overseer told it. The one called Master said it was a lie, a trick of the light. The Driver kept his mouth shut.

The slaves who could not fly told about the people who could fly to their children. When they were free. When they sat close before the fire in the free land, they told it. They did so love firelight and *Free-dom*, and tellin.

They say that the children of the ones who could not fly told their children. And now, me, I have told it to you.

The People

The Evolution of a Tale

"The People Could Fly" is a fantasy tale handed down to us from the earliest times of the Plantation Era of slavery. Told first by those slaves who never had the chance to escape from bondage, it is one of the most moving stories to be found in African American folklore.

My investigations into the subject (my research) suggest that "The People Could Fly" is a very old tale. African words are used to help tell the story. This word usage was the way the first slaves were able to keep some of their language. They were forbidden to speak their languages on the plantations, so they put African words in a tale in order to remember and preserve them. Moreover, African words were used to "make magic," which shows how much the first African Americans valued their language, culture, and heritage.

I wanted my presentation of "The People Could Fly" tale to sound well out loud and also to read well. It should reflect the ease with words the early storytellers had as they gossiped together after the

Could FLY

by Virginia Hamilton

day's work was done. They invented all kinds of tales out of the experiences of their lives.

For my written version of "The People Could Fly" story, I devised a "voice" or narrator to tell the story. The narrator "voice" sets the mood of the tale and is meant to be of the same tradition as the "voice" of the early storyteller who may have first told the story. Indeed, we realize by the end of the story that the "voice" narrator is descended from this earlier teller. In this way, I, the writer, join the past to the present. I connect the age-old teller of this tale and his or her listeners to me and my readers/listeners.

Through my reading of Black folklore, I came across many mentions of flying people. In one collection of slave narratives in which actual slaves tell about their lives in Georgia, there are more than two hundred references to flying Africans. I followed the trail of flying people through Black folklore. And I uncovered this fragment of "The People Could Fly":

"My gran says there was an ole man owned some slaves and he worked 'em hard. One day they was hoein in the field and the overseer came out and a couple of them was under a tree in the shade. And the hoe was workin by itself. The overseer said, 'What is this?' And the slaves say, 'Kum buba yali, kum buba tambe, Kim Kunka yali . . . ' (and so on). Then they rose off the ground. And they flew away. Nobody ever saw them again. Some say they flew back to Africa. My gran saw that with her own eyes."*

Finally I came across a complete story.

Some of the "reality parts" of "The People Could Fly," having to do with the people's experiences, are the slaves laboring in the fields and the mother and child suffering hunger, heat, and the overseer's whip. The fantasy part has old Toby as leader and provider for his people. He speaks strange words, which cause the people to rise up from the fields and fly away. My research reveals that the word *toby* is of African origin, meaning "to make magic." I named the hero of "The People Could Fly" Toby and the heroine Sarah. In the original tale and in the fragments, they have no names.

My task was to find a way to tell this age-old tale that would be true both to me as a storyteller and to the past storyteller. I wanted young people today to understand the horrors of slavery and to feel for those human beings, long gone, who often spent their whole lives in bondage. I think I have done so through my writing, showing that we are all part of the human condition. We all belong to one race—the human race.

Virginia Hamilton

*Somewhat paraphrased, from *Drums and Shadows: Survival Studies Among the Georgia Coastal Negroes*, Georgia Writers' Project. University of Georgia Press, 1940. Reprinted, Greenwood Press, 1973, p. 79.

Thinking About It

1 The people could fly! The story says so. Why did they make up such a story and tell it to each other?

2 Go back and find out exactly *how* people fly in this story. Try describing exactly how they do it.

3 This is a folk tale, told over and over. How can you read it or tell it so that people would want to hear it over and over? How has the author helped you know how to tell it?

Words Free as Confetti

by Pat Mora

Words, in your every color,
tumble free in my mouth,
I'll toss you in storm or breeze.

I'll say, say, say you,
taste you sweet as plump plums,
bitter as old lemons.

I'll sniff you, words, warm
as almonds or tart as apple-red,
feel you green
and soft as new grass,
lightwhite as dandelion plumes,
or thorngray as cactus,
heavy as black cement,
cold as blue icicles,
warm as *abuelita's* yellowlap.

I'll hear you, words, loud as searoar's
purple crash, hushed
as kitten curled in sleep,
as the last, goldlullaby.

I'll see you long and dark as tunnels,
bright as rainbows,
playful as chestnutwind.

I'll watch you, words, rise and dance and spin.

I'll say, say, say you
in English,
in Spanish
I'll find you.
Hold you.
Toss you.
I'm free too.
I say *yo,* I
soy, am
libre, free
free, free, free as confetti.

Fall Leaves and Poems

by Pat Mora

What is your favorite season of the year? I didn't like fall very much until I moved to the Midwest where there are trees and trees and trees.

I grew up in the Southwest and am used to cactus, deserts, mountains. Fall is beautiful in tree country. Fat, lazy leaves drift down hour after hour. They decorate sidewalks, cars, even people.

One day last fall I was taking a walk near my apartment. I started noticing all the colors I was seeing, the swirling leaves. Sometimes when I walk alone, I begin to loosen up for writing. As I walk, I let myself think about all kinds of ideas.

Pat Mora with daughters Libby and Cissy

I relax with the words inside my head. I listen to them and play with them.

As I walked, I started thinking about being bilingual, about how lucky I am to speak English and Spanish. I thought that words were like all the leaves I was seeing. They come in many shapes and sizes. They move freely through the air. Somehow I started thinking about confetti and how it swirls. I thought, "Someday, I'm going to write a book of poems for young readers and title it *Confetti*. Confetti is free and varied. It means good times and laughter."

I thought about throwing confetti, about how it feels to take a handful of color and toss it into the air. Then I thought about what it feels like to toss words into the air, in English and Spanish. I started thinking about how words taste in my mouth. Does that seem like a silly thought? Sometimes we need what may seem like silly thoughts—they're really unusual thoughts—to be able to write or say or draw an interesting idea. We have to trust our curiosity.

I like the sound of words, so once I have an idea for a poem or story, I begin to put words together to hear how they sound together. That afternoon I played a sound game as I walked, trying combinations to keep the poem from being limp and boring. I liked the sound and the mental picture, for example, of "plump plums." I liked the way the words felt in my mouth when I said them: "plump plums." I'm also interested in the rhythm of a poem. Today not all poems rhyme or have a set beat as they once did, but most of the poems I like have rhythm. I remembered games that began, "Say, say, say," and I tucked that rhythm into the poem I was beginning to write.

I decided it was time to return home and sit down with paper and pen. Now you might want to stop me here and ask, "Why would anyone sit alone and write when she could continue her walk or go have pizza with a friend?"

There are many answers. I write because I'm a reader. I want to give to others what writers have given me, a chance to hear the voices of people I will never meet. Alone, in private. It's delicious to curl up with a book.

I write because I'm curious. I'm curious about me. Writing is a way of finding out how I feel about anything and everything. Now that I've left the desert where I grew up, for example, I'm discovering how it feels to walk on those spongy fall leaves and to watch winter snow drifting *up* on a strong wind. I notice what's around me in a special way because I'm a writer, and then I talk to myself about it on paper. Writing is my way of saving my feelings.

I write because I believe that Mexican Americans need to take their place in American literature. We need to be published and to be studied at schools and colleges so that the stories and ideas of our people won't quietly disappear.

Would you like to be a writer? There are no secrets to good writing. Read. Listen. Write. Read. Listen. Write.

Sometimes a poem or story starts the way it did that fall afternoon when I began writing "Words Free as Confetti." It starts with what I'm seeing.

Sometimes a poem starts when I hear a story I want to save. Usually I like to begin writing in a sunny spot with a yellow, lined tablet and a pen. I start and stop, write and stop. I'm working but having fun. Alone. The first line of a poem or story is sometimes a hard one because I want it to be an interesting line. It may be the only line a reader will glance at before closing the book. I'm searching for the right beginning. I play a little game with myself. (This game works with any kind of writing.) I tell myself to write any line no matter how dull, since I can decide later to throw it away. If I sit waiting for the perfect line, I might never write the poem. So I start, usually slowly. I write a few lines, read them aloud, and often start again. I keep sections I like. The next day I read my work and try to improve it. I'm trying to pull out of myself the poem or story that's deep inside.

When I wrote "Words Free as Confetti," I sat down to write with an idea I liked and with some sounds and rhythms I'd been playing with as I walked on that fall day. Next I needed pictures to share with my readers. I always want careful readers to see clearly what I'm describing. I take time to combine words in ways that I hope will toss a picture right into the reader's mind. For example, can you see "old lemons"? Can you see the thick, yellow, wrinkled peel? What kind of word would be "bitter as old lemons"?

I am lucky to be a writer. So many women in history and even today who could be much better writers than I am have not had that private pleasure of creating with words.

I hope that you will want to write your own poems or songs or stories. Maybe they will be about your grandmother or about your cat or about a scientist who can make parents disappear (for just a few hours, of course). I hope that you write and that you discover what you have to say that no one else can say. Others can write *their* poems or stories, but no one, no one but you, can write yours.

POEMS FOR TWO VOICES

joyful

Noise

by Paul Fleischman

Grasshoppers

Sap's rising

Grasshoppers are
hatching out
Autumn-laid eggs

Young stepping

Ground's warming
Grasshoppers are
hatching out

splitting

into spring

Grasshoppers	Grasshoppers
hopping	hopping
high	
Grassjumpers	Grassjumpers
jumping	jumping
	far
Vaulting from	
leaf to leaf	
stem to stem	leaf to leaf
plant to plant	stem to stem
	Grass-
leapers	leapers
Grass-	
bounders	bounders
	Grass-
springers	springers
Grass-	
soarers	soarers
Leapfrogging	Leapfrogging
longjumping	longjumping
grasshoppers.	grasshoppers.

fireflies

Light

Night
is our parchment

fireflies
flitting

fireflies
glimmering

glowing

Insect calligraphers
practicing penmanship

Six-legged scribblers
of vanishing messages,

Fine artists in flight
adding dabs of light

Signing the June nights
as if they were paintings

flickering
fireflies
fireflies.

Light
is the ink we use
Night

We're
fireflies

flickering

flashing

fireflies
gleaming

Insect calligraphers

copying sentences
Six-legged scribblers

fleeting graffiti
Fine artists in flight

bright brush strokes
Signing the June nights
as if they were paintings
We're
fireflies
flickering
fireflies.

MAKING
a Joyful Noise

BY PAUL FLEISCHMAN

I was raised to tell not just the truth but the whole truth. So when I'm asked where I got the idea to write poems for two voices about insects, I reply that it came from taking piano lessons, seeing a musical score, listening to my shortwave radio, looking through trash cans, making sculptures from sticks, and taking a 2,000-mile bike ride.

I began taking piano lessons in second grade. I especially liked playing duets with my teacher or another pupil. It was exciting to see four hands moving over the keys and to hear the sound produced by twenty fingers.

Some years later, my father brought home from the library the musical score to Tchaikovsky's *Romeo and Juliet*. A score is what a composer writes and what a conductor looks at when leading an orchestra. It shows what's being played by all the instruments. My father put *Romeo and Juliet* on the stereo, and we followed along on the score with our fingers while the music flew by. I was entranced. I wanted to be a composer, to be able to hear twenty-five different instruments in my head at the same time, to carefully weave their sounds together. I wanted to write my own scores.

When I was ten, I got a shortwave radio that brought in stations from around the world. Though we lived in Santa Monica, California, I grew up listening to Radio Tokyo and Radio Havana and to dozens of other exotic stations. I didn't speak Japanese or Spanish or Czech or any of the other languages I was hearing. When you listen to a language you don't understand, you hear the language's sound, not its sense. Spoken words, I realized, had a music all their own.

My other favorite pastimes were looking through trash cans and making little houses and other creations out of sticks, pine needles, or whatever was at hand. Both of these might seem a waste of time to some, but in fact they both helped me in my writing.

When I was nineteen, I decided it was time to see the world beyond California. I rode north to

Vancouver on my bicycle, took the train across Canada, and ended up living in a 200-year-old house in the woods of New Hampshire. I'd never lived in the country before. I saw my first fireflies, heard my first cicadas, and studied with great excitement the birds and bugs and trees and flowers all around.

What does all this have to do with *Joyful Noise?* My piano duets showed me that playing music with someone else was much more fun than playing alone. Though I eventually decided that I didn't have the talent to compose musical scores, my poems for two voices are very much like duets. The music in this case comes from spoken words, not musical notes, just as it did on the shortwave radio.

Insects have lives as varied as our own. I knew this from my years in

New Hampshire, but I had to learn more before writing about them. Looking through trash cans had been my introduction to the art of research. To look through someone's trash is to look into a life. Archaeologists spend their careers doing this. Like many writers, I often snoop among people's published letters and diaries to learn more about a period or place. Making sculptures from cast-off objects is something I still do. What can you make out of a handful of sticks? How can you connect a half-dozen characters? In both cases you design, doodle, improvise, alter, experiment, and erase—all of which I did in writing *Joyful Noise.*

May you have as much fun performing these poems as I had in writing them.

Paul Fleischman

THINKING
ABOUT
IT

Think about the writers you have just read—Pat Mora and Paul Fleischman. Where do they get their ideas? Do you get your ideas for stories and poems the same way these writers do? Where do your ideas come from?

Which of these two writers would you like to work with on a writing project? What qualities about their work do you admire? What qualities about your own work do you think your "partner" would find interesting?

Suppose that Pat Mora and Paul Fleischman were painters or dancers instead of writers. Do you think the ways they get their ideas for their works would change? Explain.

A BOOK ABOUT WRITING

How to Read and Write Poetry, by Anna Cosman, will give you tips on how to get ideas and how to express yourself when you want to write poems.

THE Cat AND THE Golden Egg

by Lloyd Alexander

uickset, a silver-gray cat, lived with Dame Agnes, a poor widow. Not only was he a cheerful companion, but clever at helping the old woman make ends meet. If the chimney smoked, he tied a bundle of twigs to his tail, climbed up the flue, and cleaned it with all the skill of the town sweep. He sharpened the old woman's knives and scissors, and mended her pots and pans neatly as any tinker. Did Dame Agnes knit, he held the skein of yarn; did she spin, he turned the spinning wheel.

Now, one morning Dame Agnes woke up with a bone-cracking rheumatism. Her joints creaked, her back

ached, and her knees were so stiff she could no way get out of bed.

"My poor Quickset," she moaned, "today you and I must both go hungry."

At first, Quickset thought Dame Agnes meant it was the rheumatism that kept her from cooking breakfast, so he answered:

"Go hungry? No, indeed. You stay comfortable; I'll make us a little broiled sausage and soft-boiled egg, and brew a pot of tea for you. Then I'll sit on your lap to warm you, and soon you'll be good as new."

Before Dame Agnes could say another word, he hurried to the pantry. But, opening the cupboard, he saw only bare shelves: not so much as a crust of bread or crumb of cheese; not even a dry bone or bacon rind.

"Mice!" he cried. "Eaten every scrap! They're out of hand, I've been too easy on them. I'll settle accounts with those fellows later. But now, Mistress, I had best go to Master Grubble's market and buy what we need."

Dame Agnes thereupon burst into tears. "Oh, Quickset, it isn't mice, it's money. I have no more. Not a penny left for food or fuel."

"Why, Mistress, you should have said something about that before now," replied Quickset. "I never would have let you come to such a state. No matter, I'll think of a way to fill your purse again. Meantime, I'll have Master Grubble give us our groceries on credit."

"Grubble? Give credit?" Dame Agnes exclaimed. "You know the only things he gives is short weight at high prices. Alas for the days when the town had a dozen tradesmen and more: a baker, a butcher, a greengrocer, and all the others. But they're gone, thanks to Master Grubble. One by one, he's gobbled them up. Schemed and swindled them out of their businesses! And now he's got the whole town under his thumb, for it's deal with

Grubble or deal with no one."

"In that case," replied Quickset, "deal with him I will. Or, to put it better, he'll deal with me."

The old woman shook her head. "You'll still need money. And you shall have it, though I must do something I hoped I'd never have to do.

"Go to the linen chest," Dame Agnes went on. "At the bottom, under the good pillowslips, there's an old wool stocking. Fetch it out and bring it to me."

Puzzled, Quickset did as she asked. He found the stocking with a piece of string tied around the toe and carried it to Dame Agnes, who undid the knot, reached in and drew out one small gold coin.

"Mistress, that's more than enough," said Quickset. "Why did you fret so? With this, we can buy all we want."

Instead of being cheered by the gold piece in her hand, Dame Agnes only sighed:

"This is the last of the small savings my dear husband left to me. I've kept it all these years, and promised myself never to spend it."

"Be glad you did keep it," said Quickset, "for now's the time you need it most."

"I didn't put this by for myself," Dame Agnes replied. "It was for you. I meant to leave it to you in my will. It was to be your legacy, a little something until you found another home. But I see I shall have to spend it. Once gone, it's gone, and that's the end of everything."

At this, Dame Agnes began sobbing again. But Quickset reassured her:

"No need for tears. I'll see to this matter. Only let me have that gold piece a little while. I'll strike such a bargain with Master Grubble that we'll fill our pantry with meat and drink aplenty. Indeed he'll beg me to keep the money and won't ask a penny, that I promise."

"Master Grubble, I fear, will be more than a match even for you," Dame Agnes replied. Nevertheless, she did as Quickset urged, put the coin in a leather purse, and hung it around his neck.

uickset hurried through town to the market, where he found Master Grubble sitting on a high stool behind the counter. For all that his shelves were loaded with victuals of every kind, with meats, and vegetables, and fruits, Grubble looked as though he had never sampled his own wares. There was more fat on his bacon than on himself. He was lean-shanked and sharp-eyed, his nose narrow as a knife blade. His mouth was pursed and puckered as if he had been sipping vinegar, and his cheeks as mottled as moldy cheese. At sight of Quickset, the storekeeper never so much as climbed down from his stool to wait on his customer, but only made a sour face; and, in a voice equally sour, demanded:

"And what do you want? Half a pound of mouse tails? A sack of catnip? Out! No loitering! I don't cater to the cat trade."

Despite this curdled welcome, Quickset bowed and politely explained that Dame Agnes was ailing and he had come shopping in her stead.

"Sick she must be," snorted Master Grubble, "to send a cat marketing, without even a shopping basket. How do you mean to carry off what you buy? Push it along the street with your nose?"

"Why, sir," Quickset answered, "I thought you might send your shop boy around with the parcels. I'm sure you'll do it gladly when you see the handsome order to be filled. Dame Agnes needs a joint of beef, a shoulder of mutton, five pounds of your best sausage, a dozen of the largest eggs—"

"Not so fast," broke in the storekeeper. "Joints and shoulders, is it? Sausage and eggs? Is that what you want? Then I'll tell you what I want: cash on the counter, paid in full. Or you, my fine cat, won't have so much as a wart from one of my pickles."

"You'll be paid," Quickset replied, "and very well paid. But now I see your prices, I'm not sure I brought enough money with me."

"So that's your game!" cried Grubble. "Well, go and get enough. I'll do business with you then, and not before."

"It's a weary walk home and back again," said Quickset. "Allow me a minute or two and I'll have money to spare. And, Master Grubble, if you'd be so kind as to lend me an egg."

"Egg?" retorted Grubble. "What's that to do with paying my bill?"

"You'll see," Quickset answered. "I guarantee you'll get all that's owing to you."

Grubble at first refused and again ordered Quickset from the shop. Only when the cat promised to pay double the price of the groceries, as well as an extra fee for the

use of the egg, did the storekeeper grudgingly agree.

Taking the egg from Master Grubble, Quickset placed it on the floor, then carefully settled himself on top of it.

"Fool!" cried Grubble. "What are you doing? Get off my egg! This cat's gone mad and thinks he's a chicken!"

uickset said nothing, but laid back his ears and waved his tail, warning Grubble to keep silent. After another moment, Quickset got up and brought the egg to the counter:

"There, Master Grubble, that should be enough."

"What?" shouted the storekeeper. "Idiot cat! You mean to pay me with my own egg?"

"With better than that, as you'll see," answered Quickset. While Grubble fumed, Quickset neatly cracked the shell and poured the contents into a bowl. At this, Grubble ranted all the more:

"Alley rabbit! Smash my egg, will you? I'll rub your nose in it!"

Suddenly Master Grubble's voice choked in his gullet. His eyes popped as he stared into the bowl. There, with the broken egg, lay a gold piece.

Instantly, he snatched it out. "What's this?"

"What does it look like?" returned Quickset.

Grubble squinted at the coin, flung it onto the counter and listened to it ring. He bit it, peered closer, turned it round and round in his fingers, and finally blurted:

"Gold!"

Grubble, in his fit of temper, had never seen Quickset slip the coin from the purse and deftly drop it into the bowl. Awestruck, he gaped at the cat, then lowered his voice to a whisper:

"How did you do that?"

u i c k s e t merely shook his head and shrugged his tail. At last, as the excited storekeeper pressed him for an answer, he winked one eye and calmly replied:

"Now, now, Master Grubble, a cat has trade secrets just as a storekeeper. I don't ask yours, you don't ask mine. If I told you how simple it is, you'd know as much as I do. And if others found out—"

"Tell me!" cried Grubble. "I won't breathe a word to a living soul. My dear cat, listen to me," he hurried on. "You'll have all the victuals you want. For a month! A year! Forever! Here, this very moment, I'll have my boy

take a carload to your mistress. Only teach me to sit on eggs as you did."

"Easily done," said Quickset. "But what about that gold piece?"

"Take it!" cried Grubble, handing the coin to Quickset. "Take it, by all means."

uickset pretended to think over the bargain, then answered:

"Agreed. But you must do exactly as I tell you."

Grubble nodded and his eyes glittered. "One gold piece from one egg. But what if I used two eggs? Or three, or four, or five?"

"As many as you like," said Quickset. "A basketful, if it suits you."

Without another moment's delay, Grubble called his boy from the storeroom and told him to deliver all that Quickset ordered to the house of Dame Agnes. Then, whimpering with pleasure, he filled his biggest basket with every egg in the store. His nose twitched, his hands trembled, and his usually sallow face turned an eager pink.

"Now," said Quickset, "so you won't be disturbed, take your basket to the top shelf and sit on it there. One thing more, the most important. Until those eggs hatch, don't say a single word. If you have anything to tell me, whatever the reason, you must only cluck like a chicken. Nothing else, mind you. Cackle all you like; speak but once, and the spell is broken."

"What about my customers? Who's to wait on them?" asked Grubble, unwilling to lose business even in exchange for a fortune.

"Never fear," said Quickset. "I'll mind the store."

"What a fine cat you are," purred Grubble. "Noble animal. Intelligent creature."

With that, gleefully chuckling and licking his lips, he clambered to the top shelf, hauling his heavy burden along with him. There he squatted gingerly over the basket, so cramped that he was obliged to draw his knees under his chin and fold his arms as tightly as he could; until indeed he looked much like a skinny, long-beaked chicken hunched on a nest.

Below, Quickset no sooner had taken his place on the stool than Mistress Libbet, the carpenter's wife, stepped through the door.

"Why, Quickset, what are you doing here?" said she. "Have you gone into trade? And can that be Master Grubble on the shelf? I swear he looks as if he's sitting on a basket of eggs."

"Pay him no mind," whispered Quickset. "He fancies himself a hen. An odd notion, but harmless. However, since Master Grubble is busy nesting, I'm tending shop for him. So, Mistress Libbet, how may I serve you?"

"There's so much our little ones need." Mistress Libbet sighed unhappily. "And nothing we can afford to

feed them. I was hoping Master Grubble had some scraps or trimmings."

"He has much better," said Quickset, pulling down one of the juiciest hams and slicing away at it with Grubble's carving knife. "Here's a fine bargain today: only a penny a pound."

Hearing this, Master Grubble was about to protest, but caught himself in the nick of time. Instead, he began furiously clucking and squawking:

"Cut-cut-cut! Aw-cut!"

"What's that you say?" Quickset glanced up at the agitated storekeeper and cupped an ear with his paw. "Cut more? Yes, yes, I understand. The price is still too high? Very well, if you insist: two pounds for a penny."

Too grateful to question such generosity on the part of Grubble, Mistress Libbet flung a penny onto the counter and seized her ham without waiting for Quickset to wrap it. As she hurried from the store, the tailor's wife and the stonecutter's daughter came in; and, a moment later, Dame Gerton, the laundrywoman.

"Welcome, ladies," called Quickset. "Welcome, one and all. Here's fine prime meats, fine fresh vegetables on sale today. At these prices, they won't last long. So, hurry! Step up!"

As the delighted customers pressed eagerly toward the counter, Master Grubble's face changed from sallow to crimson, from crimson to purple. Cackling frantically, he waggled his head and flapped his elbows against his ribs.

"Cut-aw-cut!" he bawled. "Cut-cut-aw! Cuck-cuck! Cock-a-doodle-do!"

Once more, Quickset made a great show of listening carefully:

"Did I hear you a-right, Master Grubble? Give all? Free? What a generous soul you are."

With that, Quickset began hurling meats, cheese, vegetables, and loaves of sugar into the customers' outstretched baskets. Grubble's face now turned from purple to bilious green. He crowed, clucked, brayed, and bleated until he sounded like a barnyard gone mad.

"Give more?" cried Quickset. "I'm doing my best!"

"Cut-aw!" shouted Grubble and away went a chain of sausages. "Ak-ak-cut-aak!" And away went another joint of beef. At last, he could stand no more:

"Stop! Stop!" he roared. "Wretched cat! You'll drive me out of business!"

Beside himself with fury, Master Grubble forgot his cramped quarters and sprang to his feet. His head struck the ceiling and he tumbled back into the basket of eggs. As he struggled to free himself from the flood of shattered yolks, the shelf cracked beneath him and he went plummeting headlong into a barrel of flour.

"Robber!" stormed Grubble, crawling out and shaking a fist at Quickset. "Swindler! You promised I'd hatch gold from eggs!"

"What's that?" put in the tailor's wife. "Gold from eggs? Master Grubble, you're as foolish as you're greedy."

"But a fine cackler," added the laundry woman, flapping her arms. "Let's hear it again, your cut-cut-awk!"

"I warned you not to speak a word," Quickset told the storekeeper, who was egg-soaked at one end and floured at the other. "But you did. And so you broke the spell. Why, look at you, Master Grubble. You nearly turned yourself into a dipped pork chop. Have a care. Someone might fry you."

With that, Quickset went home to breakfast.

As for Master Grubble, when word spread that he had been so roundly tricked, and so easily, he became such a laughingstock that he left town and was never seen again. At the urging of the townsfolk, Dame Agnes and Quickset took charge of the market, and ran it well and fairly. All agreed that Quickset was the cleverest cat in the world. And, since Quickset had the same opinion, it was surely true.

Fun+Fancy=Fantasy

by Lloyd Alexander

Lloyd Alexander

Whenever I catch myself doing something foolish, or silly, or just plain dumb—which happens quite a lot—I imagine one of my cats observing me, shaking his head and saying to himself, "Well, there he goes again. What do you expect? After all, he's a human." I can see his point. Would any cat ever dream of behaving as unreasonably as we humans often do? I doubt it. Cats, I like to think, have more common sense than the rest of us.

Playing with that idea led to writing "The Cat and the Golden Egg" and other stories in a book called *The Town Cats*. I've always loved our household of cats, and I've always loved fairy tales. I thought it would be fun to put both of my affections together; and, indeed, so it turned out to be.

The tales are fantasies, of course. But in the kingdom of our imagination everything is possible. There, cats are able to talk, play chess, paint portraits, outwit greedy shopkeepers and thieving officials. Their human companions take all this as perfectly natural. In the realm of fairy tales, that's simply how things are.

Part of my own delight in writing the book was creating a different personality for each of the cats involved and a different atmosphere for each of the tales. For example, there's an Italian-flavored story, a French one, another with a Dutch background. "The Cat and the Golden Egg" I see as taking place in a kind of old English country town.

In addition to imagining different backgrounds, what delighted me even more was poking a little fun at some of our human foibles and frailties. In "The Cat and the Golden Egg," for instance, Master Grubble is so

carried away by the prospect of an instant golden fortune that he gladly does every nonsensical thing that Quickset suggests—and ends up making himself a laughingstock. Master Grubble is fooled not so much by a clever cat as by his own greediness. Other tales deal with pompous, self-important town councillors, a gullible shoemaker, a king whose every extravagant whim is a command and who has never been told "No" until a wise bazaar cat speaks that forbidden word to him.

Fairy tales? Yes, surely. Or, perhaps not. The stories aren't really about cats. They're about people. Not "Once upon a time," but here and now. They're told with affectionate spoofing and a great deal of tongue in cheek. But serious things can also be funny, just as funny things can also be serious.

The resourceful, quick-witted cats are, I hope, colorful characters in their own right, able to solve the knottiest problems in surprising ways and to help out the befuddled human beings. More important, however, they represent common sense, reason, goodheartedness. That is, our own best qualities which we sometimes forget.

Even so, the main purpose of "The Cat and the Golden Egg," like that of other tales, is to give pleasure to readers. And to the author; for authors are allowed to enjoy themselves too. I admit that I laughed a lot when I was writing the stories. I also realized that it's possible to laugh and learn something at the same time.

One marvelous thing about human beings is our ability to laugh. Better yet, to laugh at ourselves. If that helps us grow a little wiser, and a little kinder to each other, could any fairy tale have a happier ending?

Thinking About It

1

Quickset behaves more like a person than a cat. Have you ever known a dog or cat that seemed more like a person than an animal? Explain.

2

Do you think Master Grubble was treated harshly, fairly, or too kindly by Quickset? Explain.

3

Make up an end note to "The Cat and the Golden Egg." Imagine what has happened to Quickset, Dame Agnes, and Master Grubble one year after this tale ends.

Another Book by Lloyd Alexander

Read about more unusual cats that Lloyd Alexander has created in *The Town Cats and Other Tales*.

THE Rascal Crow

by Lloyd Alexander

Medwyn, ancient guardian and protector of animals, one day sent urgent word for the birds and beasts to join in council with him. So from lair and burrow, nest and hive, proud stag and humble mole, bright-winged eagle and drab wren, they hastened to his valley. No human could have found or followed the secret path to this shelter, for only creatures of field and forest had knowledge of it.

There they gathered, every kind and degree, one from each clan and tribe. Before them stood Medwyn garbed in a coarse brown robe, his white beard reaching to his waist, his white hair about his shoulders, his only ornament a golden band, set with a blue gem, circling his weathered brow. He spread his gnarled and knotted arms in welcome to the waiting council.

"You know, all of you," he began, in a clear voice unweakened by his years, "long ago, when the dark

waters flooded Prydain, I built a ship and carried your forefathers here to safety. Now I must warn you: your own lives are threatened."

Hearing this, the animals murmured and twittered in dismay. But Kadwyr the crow flapped his glossy wings, clacked his beak, and gaily called out:

"What, more wind and water? Let the ducks have the joy of it! Don't worry about me. My nest is high and strong enough. I'll stay where I am. Good sailing to all web-feet!"

Chuckling, making loud, impudent quackings at the blue teal, Kadwyr would have flown off then and there. Medwyn summoned him back, saying:

"Ah, Kadwyr, you're as great a scamp as your grandsire who sailed with me. No, it is neither flood nor storm. The danger is far worse. King Arawn, Lord of the Land of Death, seeks to enslave all you forest creatures, to break you to his will and bind you to serve his evil ends. Those cousins to the eagles, the gentle gwythaints, have already fallen prey to him. Arawn has lured them to his realm and trapped them in iron cages. Alas, they are beyond our help. We can only grieve for them.

"Take warning from their fate," Medwyn continued. "For now the Death-Lord sends his Chief Huntsman to bait and snare you, to bring you

captive to the Land of Death or to slaughter you without mercy. Together you must set your plans to stand against him."

"A crow's a match for any hunter," said Kadwyr. "Watch your step, the rest of you, especially you slow-footed cud-chewers."

Medwyn sighed and shook his head at the brash crow. "Even you, Kadwyr, may be glad for another's help."

Kadwyr only shrugged his wings and cocked a bold eye at Edyrnion the eagle, who flew to perch on Medwyn's outstretched arm.

"Friend of eagles," Edyrnion said, "I and my kinsmen will keep watch from the sky. Our eyes are keen, our wings are swift. At first sight of the hunter, we will spread the alarm."

"Mind you, don't fly too close to the sun," put in Kadwyr with a raucous chuckle. "You'll singe your pinfeathers and moult ahead of season. If there's any watching needed, I'd best be the one to do it. I hear you're going a bit nearsighted these days."

The nimble crow hopped away before the eagle could call him to account for his teasing. And now the gray wolf Brynach came to crouch at Medwyn's feet, saying:

"Friend of wolves, I and my kinsmen will range the forest. Our teeth are sharp, our jaws are strong. Should the hunter come among us, let him beware of our wolf packs."

"And you'd better watch out for that long tail of yours," said Kadwyr. "With all your dashing back and forth, you're likely to get burrs in it. In fact, you might do well to leave all that roving and roaming to me. My beak's as sharp as any wolf's tooth. And," the crow added, winking, "I never have to stop and scratch fleas."

The wolf's golden eyes flashed and he looked ready to teach the crow a lesson in manners. But he kept his temper and sat back on his haunches as Gwybeddin the gnat flew close to Medwyn's ear and bravely piped up:

"Friend of gnats! We are a tiny folk, but we mean to do our best in any way we can."

Hearing this, Kadwyr squawked with laughter and called out to the gnat:

"Is that you, Prince Flyspeck? I can hardly see you. Listen, old friend, the best thing you can do is hide in a dust cloud, and no hunter will ever find you. Why, even your words are bigger than you are!"

Kadwyr's remarks so embarrassed the poor gnat that he blushed and buzzed away as fast as he could. Meantime, Nedir the spider had clambered up to Medwyn's sleeve, where she clung with her long legs, and declared:

"Friend of spiders! We spinners and weavers are craftsmen, not fighters. But we shall give our help gladly wherever it is needed."

"Take my advice, Granny," Kadwyr said with a chuckle, "and keep to your knitting. Be careful you don't get your arms and legs mixed up, or you'll never untangle them."

Kadwyr hopped about and flirted his tail-feathers, croaking and cackling as the other creatures came forward one by one. The owl declared that he and his fellows would serve as night watch. The fox vowed to use his cunning to baffle the hunter and lead him on false trails. The bees pledged to wield their stings as swords and daggers. The bears offered their strength, the stags their speed, and the badgers their courage to protect their neighbors and themselves.

Last of all, plodding under his heavy burden, came Crugan-Crawgan the turtle.

"Friend of turtles," began Crugan-Crawgan in a halting voice, pondering each word, "I came . . . yes, well, that is to say I, ah, started . . . in all possible haste . . ."

"And we'll be well into next week by the time you've done telling us," Kadwyr said impatiently.

"We are . . . as I should be the first to admit . . . we are, alas, neither swift nor strong. But if I might be allowed . . . ah, permitted to state . . . we're solid. Very, very . . . solid. And . . . steady."

"Have done!" cried Kadwyr, hopping onto the turtle's shell. "You'll put me to sleep! The safest thing you can do is stay locked up in that portable castle of yours. Pull in your head! Tuck in your tail! I'll see to it the hunter doesn't batter down your walls. By the way, old fellow, didn't you have a race with a snail the other day? Tell me, who won?"

"Oh, that," replied Crugan-Crawgan. "Yes, Kadwyr, you see, what happened . . ."

Kadwyr did not wait for the turtle's answer, for Medwyn now declared the council ended, and the crow flapped away, laughing and cackling to himself. "Gnats and spiders! Turtles! What an army! I'll have to keep an eye on all of them."

Once in the forest, however, Kadwyr gave little thought to Medwyn's warning. The beavers toiled at making their dams into strongholds; the squirrels stopped up the crannies in their hollow trees; the moles dug deeper tunnels and galleries. Though every creature offered him shelter in case of need, Kadwyr shook his glossy head and answered:

"Not for me, those holes and burrows! Wits and wings! Wings and wits! There's not a crow hatched who can't get the best of any hunter!"

Soon Edyrnion and his eagle kinsmen came swooping into the forest, beating their wings and spreading the alarm. The wolf packs leaped from their lairs, the bears from their dens, the foxes from their earths, gathering to join battle against the hunter; and all the forest dwellers, each in his own way, made ready to defend nest and bower, cave and covert.

Kadwyr, however, perched on a branch, rocking back and forth, whistling gaily, daring the invader to catch him. While the smaller, weaker animals hid silent and fearful, Kadwyr hopped up and down, cawing at the top of his voice. And before the crow knew it, the hunter sprang from a thicket.

Garbed in the skins of slain animals, a long knife at his belt, a bow and quiver of arrows slung over his shoulder, the hunter had come so stealthily that Kadwyr scarcely had a moment to collect his wits. The hunter flung out a net so strong and

finely woven that once
caught in it, no creature
could hope to struggle free.

But Kadwyr's eye was
quicker than the hunter's snare.
With a taunting cackle the crow
hopped into the air, flapped his
wings, and flew from the branch to
perch higher in the tree, where he peered
down and brazenly waggled his tailfeathers.

Leaving his net, with a snarl of anger the hunter
unslung his bow, fitted an arrow to the string, and sent
the shaft hissing straight for the crow.

Chuckling, Kadwyr fluttered his wings and sailed
out of the path of the speeding arrow; then turned back
to dance in the air in front of the furious hunter, who
drew the bow again and again. Swooping and soaring, the
crow dodged every shaft.

Seeing the hunter's quiver almost empty, Kadwyr
grew even bolder, gliding closer, circling beyond reach,
then swooping back to liven the game again. Gnashing
his teeth at the elusive prey, the hunter struck out
wildly, trying to seize the nimble crow.

Kadwyr sped away. As he flew, he turned his head in
a backward glance to jeer at his defeated pursuer. In that
heedless instant, the crow collided with a tree trunk.

Stunned, Kadwyr plummeted to the ground. The
hunter ran toward him. Kadwyr croaked in pain as he
strove to fly to safety. But his wing hung useless at his
side, broken.

Breathless, Kadwyr scrambled into the bushes. The
hunter plunged after him. Earthbound and wounded,
Kadwyr began wishing he had not been so quick to turn
down shelter from the squirrels and beavers. With the

hunter gaining on him, the crow gladly would have squeezed into any tunnel, or burrow, or rabbit hole he could find. But all had been sealed, blocked, and barred with stones and twigs.

Dragging his wing, the crow skittered through the underbrush. His spindly legs were ill-suited to running, and he longed for the swiftness of the hare. He stumbled and went sprawling. An arrow buried itself in the ground beside him.

The hunter drew his bow. Though this was his pursuer's last arrow, Kadwyr knew himself a helpless target. Only a few paces away, the hunter took aim.

That same instant, a cloud of dust came whirling through the trees. Expecting in another moment to be skewered, Kadwyr now saw the hunter fling up his arms and drop his bow. The arrow clattered harmlessly into the leaves. Next, Kadwyr was sure his opponent had lost his wits. Roaring with pain, the hunter waved his arms and beat his hands against his face, trying to fend off the cloud buzzing about his head and shoulders.

The host of gnats swarmed over the raging hunter, darted into his ears and eyes, streamed up his nose and out his mouth. The more the hunter swept away the tiny creatures, the more they set upon him.

"Gwybeddin!" burst out the crow as one of the swarm broke from the cloud and lit on his beak. "Thank you for my life! Did I call you a flyspeck? You and your gnats are brave as eagles!"

"Hurry!" piped the gnat. "We're doing all we can, but he's more than a match for us. Quick, away with you!"

Kadwyr needed no urging. The gnats had saved him from the hunter's arrows and, as well, had let him snatch a moment's rest. The crow set off again as fast as he

could scramble through the dry leaves and dead branches of the forest floor.

Brave though Gwybeddin and his fellows had been, their efforts did not keep the hunter long from the chase. Soon Kadwyr heard footfalls crashing close behind him. The hunter had easily found the crow's trail and seemed to gain in strength while his prey weakened with each step.

The crow plunged deeper into the woods, hoping to hide in a heavy growth of brambles or a thicket where the hunter could not follow. Instead, to Kadwyr's dismay, the forest here grew sparser. Before the crow could find cover, the hunter sighted him and gave a triumphant shout.

Not daring another backward glance, Kadwyr scrambled through a grove of trees. The ground before him lay clear and hard-packed; but while the way was easier for him, he realized it was easier, too, for his enemy to overtake him.

Just then Kadwyr heard a bellow of rage. The crow halted to see the hunter twisting and turning, struggling as if caught in his own net. Kadwyr stared in amazement. Amid the trees, Nedir and all the spiders in the forest had joined to spin their strongest webs. The strands were so fine the hunter had not seen them, but now they clung to him, twined and wrapped around him, and the more he tried to fight loose, the more they enshrouded him.

From a branch above Kadwyr's head, sliding down a single invisible thread, came Nedir, waving her long legs.

"We spinners and weavers have done our best," she called out, "but even our stoutest webs will soon give way. Be off, while you have the chance!"

"Granny Spider," cried the grateful Kadwyr, "forgive me if I ever made sport of you. Your knitting saved my neck!"

Once again the crow scurried away, sure this time he had escaped for good and all. Despite the pain in his wing, his spirits rose and he began gleefully cackling at the sight of the hunter so enmeshed in a huge cocoon.

But Kadwyr soon snapped his beak shut. His eyes darted about in alarm, for his flight had brought him to the edge of a steep cliff.

He halted and fearfully drew back. Without the use of his wing he would have fallen like a stone and been dashed to pieces on the rocks below. However, before he could decide which way to turn, he saw the hunter racing toward him.

Free of the spiders' webs, more enraged than ever, and bent on making an end of the elusive crow, the hunter pulled his knife from his belt. With a shout of triumph, he sprang at the helpless Kadwyr.

The crow, certain his last moment had come, flapped his one good wing and thrust out his beak, bound that he would sell his life dearly.

But the hunter stumbled in midstride. His foot caught on a round stone that tripped him up and sent him plunging headlong over the cliff.

Kadwyr's terror turned to joyous relief. He cawed, cackled, and crowed as loudly as any rooster. Then his beak fell open in astonishment.

The stone that had saved his life began to sprout four stubby legs and a tail; a leathery neck stretched out cautiously, and Crugan-Crawgan, the turtle, blinked at Kadwyr.

"Are you all right?" asked Crugan-Crawgan. "That is, I mean to say . . . you've come to no harm? I'm sorry . . .

ah, Kadwyr, there wasn't more I could have . . .
done. We turtles, alas, can't run . . . like rabbits.
Or fly . . . like eagles. But we are, I hope you'll
agree . . . yes, we are solid, if nothing else. And
. . . very, very steady."

"Crugan-Crawgan," said Kadwyr, "you
saved my life and I thank you. Steady and
solid you are, old fellow, and I'm glad of it."

"By the way," the turtle went on, "as I was
saying . . . the last time we met. . . . Yes, the snail
and I did have a race. It was . . . a draw."

The forest was again safe and the rejoicing
animals came out of their hiding places. Edyrnion
the eagle bore the wounded crow to Medwyn's
valley, to be cared for and sheltered until his
wing healed.

"Ah, Kadwyr, you scamp, I didn't expect to
see you here so soon," Medwyn told the
crow, who admitted all that had happened
in the woods. "Your wing will mend and
you'll be ready for some new scrape. But
let us hope next time you can help
your friends as they helped you."

"I know better than to scorn
a spider," said Kadwyr, crestfallen. "I'll
never taunt a turtle. And never again
annoy a gnat. But—but, come to
think of it," he went on, his
eyes brightening, "if it hadn't been
for me—yes, it was I! I who led that
hunter a merry chase! I who saved all
in the forest!"

Kadwyr chuckled and clucked, bobbed his head, and snapped his beak, altogether delighted with himself.

"Perhaps you did, at that," Medwyn gently answered. "In any case, go in peace, Kadwyr. The world has room enough for a rascal crow."

Thinking About It

1

"Have you ever known a Kadwyr?" What if someone asked you that? Surely it wouldn't mean, have you ever known a crow! When you've figured out what a Kadwyr is, it's time to decide whether there's room enough in the world for Kadwyrs. What do you think?

2

If you could spend an afternoon with Lloyd Alexander, what would you like to do? What questions would you ask him about his writing?

3

Tales like "The Rascal Crow" often have morals added to their endings—a few sentences that explain what lesson is to be learned from the story. Write a moral for "The Rascal Crow."

Cinderella

Finds Time

by Val R. Cheatham

Characters

narrator

Cinderella

Fairy Godmother

PRINCE

Courtier

page

STEPMOTHER

1st STEPSISTER

2ND STEPSISTER

cl  ck

Scene 1

Setting: Kitchen in STEPMOTHER's house.

At Rise: NARRATOR enters and stands facing audience while speaking.

narrator This is the story of Cinderella, who, as you know, lives with her mean stepmother and her lazy stepsisters. While they are loafing around the castle or living it up at parties, poor Cinderella has to stay home and carry out the trash, polish the armor, and make sure all the other household chores are done. As our play begins, the stepsisters have received invitations to attend the Grand Ball at the Palace. The Prince has just returned home from the wars, and everyone wants him to get married. Now, at last, the long-awaited day of the Ball has arrived. (1ST STEPSISTER *enters, yawns, and* *slowly plods toward chair.*) So as I take my leave, we find the household in a state of breathless excitement. (*Exits.* 1ST STEPSISTER *slumps motionless into kitchen chair, her head resting in her hand. She yawns and shifts her head to rest on other hand.*)

1ˢᵗ STEPSISTER   Cinderella! Cinderella!

Cinderella   (*Entering with broom, mop, feather duster, and so forth*) Yes, Stepsister?

1ˢᵗ STEPSISTER   Shut the window. I can't stand to hear those birds sing.

Cinderella   I'll be glad to, Stepsister. (*Shuts window, then exits*)

1ˢᵗ STEPSISTER   Cinderella! Cinderella!

Cinderella   (*Entering*) Yes, Stepsister?

1ˢᵗ STEPSISTER   Open the window. It's stuffy in here.

Cinderella   Why certainly, Stepsister. (*Opens window, then exits right, as* STEPMOTHER *enters left and sees* STEPSISTER *slouched in chair.*)

STEPMOTHER   Land sakes, girl! Why aren't you getting ready for the Grand Ball, where your natural beauty and charm will captivate the Prince, and he will marry you and you will live happily ever after?

1ˢᵗ STEPSISTER (*Bored*) Hurry, hurry, hurry! That's all you think about. If I don't conserve my energy, how will I be able to dance with the Prince tonight?

STEPMOTHER But it's almost noon. That leaves only eight hours for you to get ready. By the way, where is your sister? (*She sits down.*)

1ˢᵗ STEPSISTER Up in our room.

STEPMOTHER Is she dressing?

1ˢᵗ STEPSISTER Not yet.

STEPMOTHER (*Nervously*) Why not? Doesn't she know what time it is?

1ˢᵗ STEPSISTER Last week when you saw our room in such a mess, you made the rule that the last one out of bed in the morning had to clean the room and make the bed. Remember?

STEPMOTHER Yes, I remember.

1ˢᵗ STEPSISTER Well, sister is still in bed.

STEPMOTHER Perhaps the poor dear is tired. After all, a growing girl needs plenty of rest.

1ˢᵗ STEPSISTER Yes, but a week of it?

STEPMOTHER Do you mean it's been a week since

she made the bed?

1ˢᵗ STEPSISTER No, it's been a week since she got out of bed.

STEPMOTHER We simply can't have this! It's intolerable indolence, disgraceful lethargy! I'll have Cinderella clean your room and make the bed. She can work it in between milking the cows and washing the clothes. After all, a growing girl needs plenty of exercise. (*Calls*) Cinderella! Cinderella!

Cinderella (*Entering*) Yes, Mother?

STEPMOTHER Shut the window. I can't stand hearing those birds sing.

Cinderella Of course, Mother.

STEPMOTHER And stop calling me Mother! It's *Step*mother—*Step*mother!

Cinderella Yes, *Step*mother. Anything else, *Step*mother?

STEPMOTHER Go upstairs, wake up your other stepsister and make her bed. Then help her get ready for the Grand Ball, where her natural beauty and charm will captivate the Prince, and he will marry her and they will live happily ever after!

(*Curtain*)

Setting: Same as Scene 1.

At Rise: NARRATOR enters.

narrator   There it is: Scene 1—short, yet long enough to spin the intricate web of intrigue necessary to engage the viewers in various speculations until a satisfying conclusion is reached. Of course, if you've read the story, you already know about all that. Scene 2 also takes place at the Stepmother's house—but later. After eight long hours of brushing hair and teeth, attaching eyelashes and earrings, smearing rouge and lipstick, and painting fingernails and toenails—in case they lose a slipper—Cinderella's two stepsisters, and the Stepmother, too, depart for the Grand Ball, where their natural beauty and charm will captivate the Prince, and he will marry them and they will live happily ever after. Now, on with the story! (*Exits right, as* CINDERELLA *enters left.*)

Cinderella   I've hurried through my work so fast, I've nothing left to do. (FAIRY GODMOTHER *enters right, brandishing her magic wand.*)

Fairy Godmother   (*Waving wand with flourish*) Presto—chango—alakazam . . . and Open Sesame!

Cinderella   What? Who are you?

Fairy Godmother   I am your . . . I am here to . . .
ah-h-h . . . I came to . . . I was summoned . . .
ah-h-h . . . I . . . I . . . I don't know.

Cinderella (*Pointing to wand*) A wand! I'll bet you're
my Fairy Godmother!

Fairy Godmother   Yes! That's right. I'm your Fairy
Godmother. You are Little Red Riding Hood, and
I'm here to save you from the Three Little Pigs.

Cinderella   No, I'm Cinderella.

Fairy Godmother   (*Puzzled*) Well, what *are* you doing
here with the Three Little Pigs?

Cinderella   I don't live here with the Three Little
Pigs. I live here with my stepmother and two
stepsisters. Three . . . three, ah-h-h, people.

Fairy Godmother   What happened to Little Red
Riding Hood?

Cinderella   I don't know about Little Red Riding
Hood. All I know is that I'm supposed to get a
gorgeous hairdo, a beautiful new evening gown —
with sparkly slippers to match — and a coach and
four, to take me to the Grand Ball, where my
natural beauty and charm will captivate the Prince,
and he will marry me and we'll live happily ever
after.

Fairy Godmother   So that's it. O.K. Let's start with the coach. (*Circles wand in air, pauses*) Is that a basketball or a football coach?

Cinderella   No, no! A horse-drawn coach to take me to the Ball.

Fairy Godmother   Oh, yes. I remember now. Just show me the pumpkin patch, and I'll hocus-pocus it right up.

Cinderella   What about my new clothes?

Fairy Godmother   Of course, first your gown. Let's see now, where is my wand?

Cinderella   In your hand.

Fairy Godmother   (*Raising wand and waving it in circle*) Oh, yes! Now . . . Bubble, bubble, toil and trouble . . . (*Breaking off suddenly*) By the way, what time is it?

Cinderella   I don't know. Why?

Fairy Godmother   Well, I just remembered that you have to be home at twelve o'clock. If you don't know what time it is, how will you know when to leave the ball?

Cinderella   I never thought of that.

Fairy Godmother   Let me try this wand and find out.

(*Again flourishes wand*) Bulova, Bulova, toil and Timex. Tell me—(*Knock on door is heard.*)

Cinderella Who could that be? (*Calling*) Come in! (CLOCK *enters quickly with jaunty step, snapping his fingers as he approaches* CINDERELLA.)

cl**O**ck (*Snapping his fingers to beat of popular dance step which he does*) A tick and a tock, a tick and a tock . . . It's Time, Baby, Time. (*Snaps fingers again and continues with new dance step, and rhythmical "ticking"*) Tick, tock . . . tick-tock, tick; tick, tock, tick-tock tick; tick, tock, tick-tock tick.

Cinderella Time? Time for what?

cl**O**ck Grand Ball time, chickie-baby. Let's swing! (*Continues dancing, ticking, and finger-snapping.*)

Cinderella With you?

cl**O**ck Of course, little lady. Big Mama here said you needed time and that's my bag. Let's get where it's at! (*Softly*) Tick; tick-tock. Tick-tick-tock. Tick; tick-tock.

Cinderella All right, but this sure isn't the way I thought it would be. (*To* FAIRY GODMOTHER) What about my clothes?

Fairy Godmother Just wait one minute. I'll wave my . . . (*Looks at wand in puzzlement*) my . . . my . . .

Cinderella   Wand.

Fairy Godmother   Yes, that's it—my wand! I'll wave my
wand and when I count to three you shall have
them. Ready? One—two . . . ah-h-h-h . . . two
(*Pauses*)—ah-h-h . . .

Cinderella   Three?

Fairy Godmother   (*Jumping joyfully*) Yes—THREE!

(*Curtain*)

Scene 3

Setting: *Same as Scenes 1 and 2.*

At Rise: NARRATOR *enters.*

narrator   Well, the Grand Ball is over and it was a blast. Everything started out as planned. Cinderella arrived in a gorgeous hairdo, a beautiful new evening gown, with sparkly slippers to match, and all her natural beauty and charm would have captivated the Prince right then and there, if some nutty clock had not jumped up and yelled, "Time for the Sockhop!" So-o-o, all the shoes were kicked into a big pile in the middle of the floor, and the whole crowd danced till curfew. And now we are ready for the final and summarizing scene, where we should learn the answer to the question: How will the Prince ever find the right slipper for the right foot, so he can get married and live happily ever after? Let us begin at the end. *(Exits, as* TWO STEPSISTERS *enter right. They plod across stage to chairs, plop themselves down, resting heads on hands, yawning, then shifting to rest heads on other hand, yawning from time to time.* 2ND STEPSISTER *dozes off.)*

1st STEPSISTER   *(Calling loudly)* Cinderella! Cinderella! (CINDERELLA *enters promptly.*)

Cinderella   Yes, Stepsister?

1st STEPSISTER   Shut the window. Those birds are driving me batty.

Cinderella   It would be a pleasure, Stepsister. (*Shuts window, then exits.* 1ST STEPSISTER *falls asleep, and* 2ND STEPSISTER *wakes with a start.*)

2ND STEPSISTER   Cinderella! Cinderella! (CINDERELLA *runs in.*)

Cinderella   You called, Stepsister?

2ND STEPSISTER   Can't you regulate that stupid window?

Cinderella   I'll try, Stepsister. (*Opens window and continues to stand by it, opening and closing it as directed by motions from* 2ND STEPSISTER.)

STEPMOTHER   (*Entering*) Land sakes, girls! Why aren't you getting your feet ready to fit into the slipper, so your natural beauty and charm will—

2ND STEPSISTER   Come off it, Mother! You know I'll never get these size nines into those little slippers. (*Irritably*) Cinderella, close that window!

Cinderella   Of course, Stepsister—anything to please! (*She bangs down window, and* 1ST STEPSISTER *wakes with a start.*)

STEPMOTHER   (*To* 1ST STEPSISTER) Well, it's about

time you woke up. We have plans to make so that you can get ready to fit into the slipper, so your natural beauty . . .

1ˢᵗ STEPSISTER   Maybe lying in bed for the next week, resting, would help shrink my feet. (*There is a loud knocking at the door.*)

STEPMOTHER   Cinderella, open the door. (CINDERELLA *scurries to open door, and* PRINCE *enters, followed by* COURTIER, *and* PAGE, *who has large box of shoes on large pillow.* COURTIER *holds scroll from which he reads.*)

Courtier   (*Reading*) Hear ye, hear ye! It is hereby commanded by Royal Edict that every woman who was in attendance at the Grand Ball shall have the opportunity to try on these shoes to determine who will be worthy of joining the Prince of the Realm—

STEPMOTHER   Yes! Yes! We know all that. Let's get on with the fitting! (*She rushes to box* PAGE *is carrying, grabs pair of shoes and runs to give them to* 1ST STEPSISTER, *then runs back, grabs another pair and gives them to* 2ND STEPSISTER.) Now hurry, girls. See if the shoes fit. (*They put shoes on quickly.*)

1ˢᵗ STEPSISTER   (*Holding out her feet with shoes on*) These fit perfectly.

2ᴺᴰ STEPSISTER   So do these.

Cinderella   But, Prince, does this mean that you are
going to marry *both* of them?

PRINCE   Who said anything about marrying them?
After the Ball I was left with a mountain of used
shoes. I'm recruiting an army of sales clerks to open
a whole new chain of shoe stores. (*To* COURTIER,
pointing to STEPSISTERS) These two will do!

STEPMOTHER   But what about living happily...

PRINCE   (*Breaking in and pointing to* STEPMOTHER)
You can take her along too.

Courtier   All right, now. Attention! Forward, march. Hut,
two, three, four! Hut, two, three, four! Hut, two . . .
(COURTIER *continues counting as he marches*
STEPSISTERS *and* STEPMOTHER *offstage.*)

PRINCE   (*Arms outstretched to* CINDERELLA) And now,
at last, I have time for you!

clOck   (*Rushing in*) Time! Did you say *Time?* Well,
wind me up and ring my chime! (*Snapping fingers,
he begins rhythmic dance.*) Tick, tock,tick-tock tick.
Tick, tock, tick-tock tick. And a tick, tock . . .

PRINCE   (*Embracing Cinderella*) Our love shall be
timeless.

Cinderella   (*Turning to the audience*) This has got to be
the end!

(*Quick curtain*)

Thinking About It

1   Cinderella has survived dancers, singers, storytellers, cartoonists, and poets. If there were a real Cinderella, what would she say of this new, timely version of her story? What can you do to make it a treat for Cinderella fans everywhere?

2   In a good play, actions must speak as well as words. Which actions in "Cinderella Finds Time" ought to impress the audience?

3   Select an old story — a folk tale or fairy tale. Give it a twist. Presto. You'll have a new, timely, economy-size play. Try it!

Another Cinderella Story

Mufaro's Beautiful Daughters, by John Steptoe, is a Cinderella tale set in a small village in Africa.

In Search of Cinderella

by Shel Silverstein

From dusk to dawn,
From town to town,
Without a single clue,
I seek the tender, slender foot
To fit this crystal shoe.
From dusk to dawn,
I try it on
Each damsel that I meet.
And I still love her so, but oh,
I've started hating feet.

Glass Slipper

by Jane Yolen

How silly. Glass
would cut my feet to ribbons,
little scarlet ribbons,
marking my path
all the way home.
And even if they did not break,
they would never get comfortable,
molding themselves
to the bumps and bevels of my toes.
No prince is worth the pain.
Besides—I want to dance
all night.

...And Then the Prince Put the Glass Slipper...

by Judith Viorst

I really didn't notice

that he had a funny nose.

And he certainly looked better

all dressed up in fancy clothes.

He's not nearly as attractive

as he seemed the other night.

So I think I'll just pretend that

this glass slipper feels too tight.

Yeh-Shen

A Cinderella Story from China

retold by Ai-Ling Louie
illustrated by Ed Young

In the dim past, even before the Ch'in and the Han dynasties, there lived a cave chief of southern China by the name of Wu. As was the custom in those days, Chief Wu had taken two wives. Each wife in her turn had presented Wu with a baby daughter. But one of the wives sickened and died, and not too many days after that Chief Wu took to his bed and died too.

Yeh-Shen, the little orphan, grew to girlhood in her stepmother's home. She was a bright child and lovely, too, with skin as smooth as ivory and dark pools for eyes.

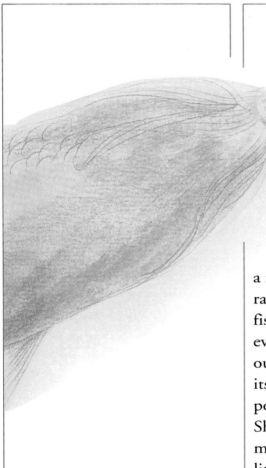

Her stepmother was jealous of all this beauty and goodness, for her own daughter was not pretty at all. So in her displeasure, she gave poor Yeh-Shen the heaviest and most unpleasant chores.

The only friend that Yeh-Shen had to her name was a fish she had caught and raised. It was a beautiful fish with golden eyes, and every day it would come out of the water and rest its head on the bank of the pond, waiting for Yeh-Shen to feed it. Step-mother gave Yeh-Shen little enough food for herself, but the orphan child always found something to share with her fish, which grew to enormous size.

Somehow the stepmother heard of this. She was terribly angry to discover that Yeh-Shen had kept a secret from her. She hurried down to the pond, but she was unable to see the fish, for Yeh-Shen's pet wisely hid itself. The stepmother, however, was a crafty woman, and she soon thought of a plan. She walked home and called out, "Yeh-Shen, go and collect some firewood. But wait! The neighbors might see you. Leave your filthy coat here!" The minute the girl was out of sight, her stepmother slipped on the coat herself and went down again to the pond. This time the big fish saw Yeh-Shen's familiar jacket and heaved itself onto the bank, expecting to be fed. But the stepmother, having hidden a dagger in her sleeve, stabbed the fish, wrapped it in her garments, and took it home to cook for dinner.

When Yeh-Shen came to the pond that evening, she found her pet had disappeared. Overcome with grief, the girl collapsed on the ground and dropped her tears into the still waters of the pond.

"Ah, poor child!" a voice said.

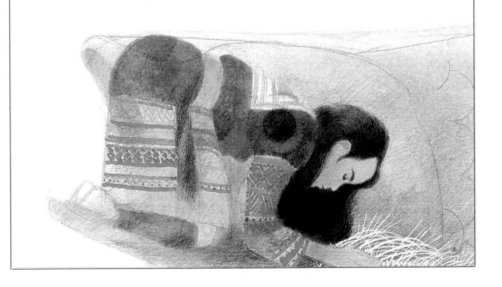

Yeh-Shen sat up to find a very old man looking down at her. He wore the coarsest of clothes, and his hair flowed down over his shoulders.

"Kind uncle, who may you be?" Yeh-Shen asked.

"That is not important, my child. All you must know is that I have been sent to tell you of the wondrous powers of your fish."

"My fish, but sir . . . " The girl's eyes filled with tears, and she could not go on.

The old man sighed and said, "Yes, my child, your fish is no longer alive, and I must tell you that your stepmother is once more the cause of your sorrow." Yeh-Shen gasped in horror, but the old man went on. "Let us not dwell on things that are past," he said, "for I have come bringing you a gift. Now you must listen carefully to this: The bones of your fish are filled with a powerful spirit. Whenever you are in serious need, you must kneel before them and let them know your heart's desire. But do not waste their gifts."

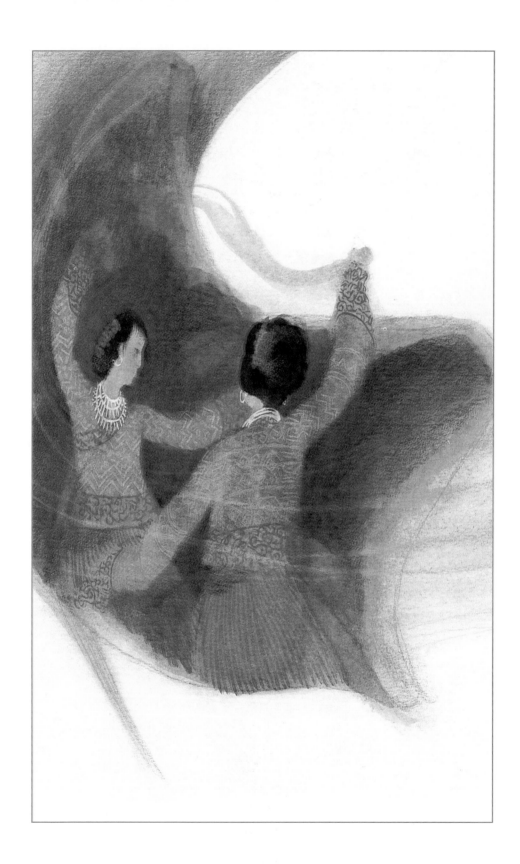

Yeh-Shen wanted to ask the old sage many more questions, but he rose to the sky before she could utter another word. With heavy heart, Yeh-Shen made her way to the dung heap to gather the remains of her friend.

Time went by, and Yeh-Shen, who was often left alone, took comfort in speaking to the bones of her fish. When she was hungry, which happened quite often, Yeh-Shen asked the bones for food. In this way, Yeh-Shen managed to live from day to day, but she lived in dread that her stepmother would discover her secret and take even that away from her.

So the time passed and spring came. Festival time was approaching: It was the busiest time of the year. Such cooking and cleaning and sewing there was to be done! Yeh-Shen had hardly a moment's rest. At the spring festival young men and young women from the village hoped to meet and to choose whom they would marry. How Yeh-Shen longed to go! But her stepmother had other plans. She hoped to find a husband for her own daughter and did not want any man to see the beauteous Yeh-Shen first. When finally the holiday arrived, the stepmother and her daughter dressed themselves in their finery and filled their baskets with sweetmeats. "You must remain at home now, and watch to see that no one steals fruit from our trees," her stepmother told Yeh-Shen, and then she departed for the banquet with her own daughter.

As soon as she was alone, Yeh-Shen went to speak to the bones of her fish. "Oh, dear friend," she said, kneeling before the precious bones, "I long to go to the festival, but I cannot show myself in these rags. Is there somewhere I could borrow clothes fit to wear to the feast?" At once she found herself dressed in a gown of azure blue, with a cloak of kingfisher feathers draped around her shoulders. Best of all, on her tiny feet were the most beautiful slippers she had ever seen. They were woven of golden threads, in a pattern like the scales of a fish, and the glistening soles were made of solid gold. There was magic in the shoes, for they should have been quite heavy, yet when Yeh-Shen walked, her feet felt as light as air.

"Be sure you do not lose your golden shoes," said the spirit of the bones. Yeh-Shen promised to be careful. Delighted with her transformation, she bid a fond farewell to the bones of her fish as she slipped off to join in the merrymaking.

That day Yeh-Shen turned many a head as she appeared at the feast. All around her people whispered, "Look at that beautiful girl! Who can she be?"

But above this, Stepsister was heard to say, "Mother, does she not resemble our Yeh-Shen?"

Upon hearing this, Yeh-Shen jumped up and ran off before her stepsister could look closely at her. She raced down the mountainside, and in doing so, she lost one of her golden slippers. No sooner had the shoe fallen from her foot than all her fine clothes turned back to rags. Only one thing remained—a tiny golden shoe.

Yeh-Shen hurried to the bones of her fish and returned the slipper, promising to find its mate. But now the bones were

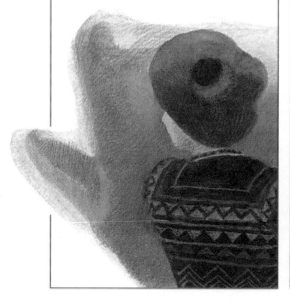
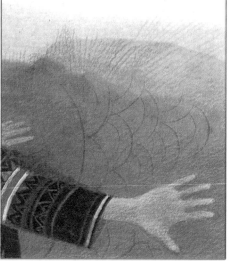

silent. Sadly Yeh-Shen realized that she had lost her only friend. She hid the little shoe in her bedstraw, and went outside to cry. Leaning against a fruit tree, she sobbed and sobbed until she fell asleep.

The stepmother left the gathering to check on Yeh-Shen, but when she returned home she found the girl sound asleep, with her arms wrapped around a fruit tree. So thinking no more of her, the step-mother rejoined the party.

Meantime, a villager had found the shoe. Recog-nizing its worth, he sold it to a merchant, who presented it in turn to the king of the island kingdom of T'o Han.

The king was more than happy to accept the slipper as a gift. He was entranced by the tiny thing, which was shaped of the most precious of metals, yet which made no sound when touched to stone. The more he marveled at its beauty, the more determined he became to find the woman to whom the shoe belonged. A search was begun among the ladies of his own

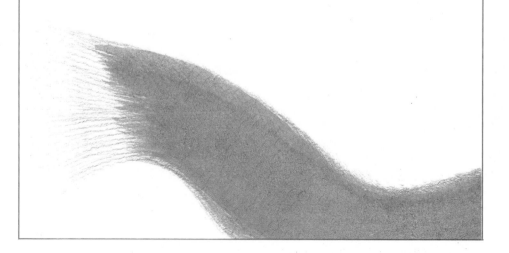

kingdom, but all who tried on the sandal found it impossibly small. Undaunted, the king ordered the search widened to include the cave women from the countryside where the slipper had been found. Since he realized it would take many years for every woman to come to his island and test her foot in the slipper, the king thought of a way to get the right woman to come forward. He ordered the sandal placed in a pavilion by the side of the road near where it had been found, and his herald announced that the shoe was to be returned to its original owner. Then from a nearby hiding place, the king and his men settled down to watch and wait for a woman with tiny feet to come and claim her slipper.

All that day the pavilion was crowded with cave women who had come to test a foot in the shoe. Yeh-Shen's stepmother and stepsister were among them, but not Yeh-Shen— they had told her to stay home. By day's end, although many women had eagerly tried to put on the slipper, it still had not been worn. Wearily, the king continued his vigil into the night.

It wasn't until the blackest part of night, while the moon hid behind a cloud, that Yeh-Shen dared to show her face at the pavilion, and even then she tiptoed timidly across the wide floor. Sinking down to her knees, the girl in rags examined the tiny shoe. Only when she was sure that this was the missing mate to her own golden slipper did she dare pick it up. At last she could return both little shoes to the fish bones. Surely then her beloved spirit would speak to her again.

Now the king's first thought, on seeing Yeh-Shen take the precious slipper, was to throw the girl into prison as a thief. But when she turned to leave, he caught a glimpse of her face. At once the king was struck by the sweet harmony of her features, which seemed so out of keeping with the rags she wore. It was then that he took a closer look and noticed that she walked upon the tiniest feet he had ever seen.

With a wave of his hand, the king signaled that this tattered creature was to be allowed to depart with the golden slipper. Quietly, the king's men slipped off and followed her home.

All this time, Yeh-Shen was unaware of the excitement she had caused. She had made her way home and was about to hide both sandals in her bedding when there was a pounding at the door. Yeh-Shen went to see who it was—and found a king at her doorstep. She was very frightened at first, but the king spoke to her in a kind voice and asked her to try the golden slippers on her feet. The maiden did as she was told, and as she stood in her golden shoes, her rags were transformed once more into the feathered cloak and beautiful azure gown.

Her loveliness made her seem a heavenly being, and the king suddenly knew in his heart that he had found his true love.

Not long after this, Yeh-Shen was married to the king. But fate was not so gentle with her stepmother and stepsister.

Since they had been unkind to his beloved, the king would not permit Yeh-Shen to bring them to his palace. They remained in their cave home, where one day, it is said, they were crushed to death in a shower of flying stones.

PULLING THE THEME TOGETHER

1

Like the Prince or King, scholars search everywhere, and everywhere they find Cinderella stories. Why? Why is the Cinderella story so widely known? Why is it in so many different versions? If you, as a scholar, found "Yeh-Shen," how would you know that it is a version of the Cinderella story?

2

Look back at the traditional tales in this book. Some are updated. Some are written in modern authors' words. At first, they seem different from each other. But here is your challenge: Figure out how they are all somehow alike. How would you define a traditional tale?

3

Now it's your turn to join the tradition. Create a modern traditional tale.

Books to Enjoy

The Korean Cinderella
by Shirley Climo
HarperCollins, 1993
The Cinderella story is found in almost every culture in the world. In this version, Cinderella is called Pear Blossom and Omoni is the jealous stepmother.

The Dollhouse Caper
by Jean O'Connell
Harper, 1976
The Dollhouse people must warn the humans that the big house is about to be robbed. Will the humans believe the Dollhouse people even exist?

Three Strong Women: A Tall Tale from Japan
by Claus Stamm
Illustrated by Jean and Mou-sien Tseng
Viking, 1990
The famous wrestler Forever Mountain thinks he is the strongest person in Japan until he meets up with a plump little girl and her mother and grandmother.

Behind the Attic Wall

by Sylvia Cassedy

Avon, 1985

Maggie has one last chance to behave. Will her aunts agree to keep her? Will the voices Maggie hears help her adjust to her new life?

I Am Phoenix

by Paul Fleischman

Harper, 1985

What is the Phoenix? Who are the Watchers? Who are the Actor and the Warblers? Sit down with this book and a friend, and find out.

The Phantom Tollbooth

by Norton Juster

Random House, 1961

Bored Milo embarks on a wondrous adventure through the Phantom Tollbooth and into the Lands Beyond, a powerhouse of puns.

Make-believe Ball Player

by Alfred Slote

Lippincott, 1989

Henry prefers playing make-believe baseball to the real game. But when real life turns dangerous, make-believing becomes a survival skill.

Literary Terms

Alliteration

Alliteration is the repetition of consonant sounds at the beginnings of words or within words. "Six-legged scribblers of vanishing messages" in "Fireflies" is an example of alliteration using the sound that the letter *s* stands for.

Fairy Tales

Like other traditional tales, **fairy tales,** like "Yeh-Shen," have been passed down from one generation to another. Many begin with "Once upon a time" because they are set long ago. Characters and events in fairy tales are often magical. No matter what terrible things happen, good almost always triumphs in the end. Evil characters, such as Yeh-Shen's stepmother and sister, are soundly punished.

Metaphor

A **metaphor** is a comparison between two things that are very different. The metaphor "light is the ink we use" in "Fireflies" calls attention to an unusual use of light. Light becomes a tool for the fireflies to write with in the dark. In "The People Could Fly," the master is described as "a hard rock pile" that couldn't be moved. Would you say he is an easy man or a difficult one after reading this metaphor?

Personification

To **personify** an animal or object is to give it human qualities. Lloyd Alexander personifies Kadwyr, the rascal crow, as arrogant and know-it-all, qualities associated with humans, not animals. Quickset, the cat who outwits Master Grubble, can speak, run a grocery store, and outwit a greedy merchant. Lloyd Alexander uses personification, not realism, to create Quickset.

Rhythm

Rhythm is a pattern of sounds created by stressed and unstressed syllables. Paul Fleischman uses rhythm in lines like "leapfrogging, longjumping grasshoppers" to translate the motion of a grasshopper's jumps into the poem.

Simile

A comparison that uses words *like* or *as* is a **simile.** In "Words Free as Confetti," Pat Mora uses many similes to create the idea that words can be tasted, smelled, felt, heard, and seen. When we read that a word is "tart as apple-red" or "warm as almonds," we have a new idea of a word, one that helps us think about a word in a new way.

Symbolism

A **symbol** is a person, place, event, or object that has an ordinary meaning but suggests other more unusual meanings as well. For example, *flight* has a very specific meaning—soaring above the earth. However, flight is also a symbol of freedom, for when a bird flies high above the earth it is free. In "The People Could Fly," the idea of flight to slaves suggests freedom.

Glossary

Vocabulary from your selections

be fud dle (bi fud′l), confuse; bewilder. *v.*, **be fud dled, be fud dling.** —**be fud′dle- ment,** *n.*

cal lig ra pher (kə lig′rə fər), person who writes by hand beautifully. *n.*

cap ti vate (kap′tə vāt), hold captive by beauty or interest; charm; fascinate: *The children were captivated by the exciting story. v.,* **cap ti vat ed, cap ti vat ing.** —**cap′ti vat′ing ly,** *adv.*

com pose (kəm pōz′), **1** make up; form: *The ocean is composed of salt water. Our party was composed of three grown-ups and four children.* **2** put together. To compose a story or poem is to construct it from words. To compose a piece of music is to invent the tune and write down the notes. To compose a picture is to arrange the things in it artistically. *v.,* **com posed, com pos ing.**

com pos er (kəm pō′zər), **1** person who composes. **2** writer of music. *n.*

com pre hend (kom′pri hend′), understand the meaning of: *If you can use a word correctly, you comprehend it. v.*

con fet ti (kən fet′ē), bits of colored paper thrown about at carnivals, weddings, or parades. *n.*

coun cil (koun′səl), **1** group of people called together to give advice and to discuss or settle questions. **2** group of persons elected by citizens to make laws for and manage a city or town. *n.*

cour ti er (kôr′tē ər), person often present at a royal court; court attendant. *n.*

craft y (kraf′tē), skillful in deceiving others; sly; tricky: *a crafty schemer. adj.,* **craft i er, craft i est.**

composer (def. 2)— Ludwig van Beethoven, 1770-1827, German **composer** of classical music

dis please (dis plēz′), not please; annoy; offend: *You displease your parents when you disobey them. v.,* **dis pleased, dis pleas ing.**

dis pleas ure (dis plezh′ər), the feeling of being displeased; annoyance; dislike. *n.*

e lude (i lüd′), **1** avoid or escape by cleverness or quickness; slip away from: *The fox eluded the dogs.* **2** remain undiscovered or unexplained by; baffle: *The answer to the problem eluded me. v.,* **e lud ed, e lud ing.**

e lu sive (i lü′siv), **1** hard to describe or understand; baffling: *I had an idea that was too elusive to put in words.* **2** tending to avoid or escape: *The elusive fox got away. adj.* —**e lu′sive ly,** *adv.*

en shroud (en shroud′), cover or hide; veil: *Fog enshrouded the ship. v.*

foi ble (foi′bəl), a weak point; weakness: *Talking too much is one of my foibles. n.*

folk lore (fōk′lôr′), beliefs, legends, customs, etc., of a people or tribe. *n.*

fore fa ther (fôr′fä′ᴛʜər), ancestor. *n.*

frail ty (frāl′tē), fault caused by weakness: *Nobody is perfect; we all have our frailties. n., pl.* **frail ties.**

gul li ble (gul′ə bəl), easily deceived or cheated. *adj.*

hal lu ci na tion (hə lü′sn ā′shən), **1** a seeing or hearing things that exist only in a person's imagination. **2** an imaginary thing seen or heard. *n.*

im merse (i mèrs′), **1** dip or lower into a liquid until covered by it: *I immersed my aching feet in a bucket of hot water.* **2** involve deeply; absorb: *The young pianist immersed herself in practice seven days a week. v.,* **im mersed, im mers ing.**

jeal ous (jel′əs), full of envy; envious: *She is jealous of her sister's good grades. adj.* —**jeal′ous ly,** *adv.*

knot ty (not′ē), **1** full of knots: *knotty wood.* **2** difficult; puzzling: *a knotty problem. adj.,* **knot ti er, knot ti est.**

a	hat	oi	oil
ā	age	ou	out
ä	far	u	cup
e	let	ů	put
ē	equal	ü	rule
ėr	term		
i	it	ch	child
ī	ice	ng	long
o	hot	sh	she
ō	open	th	thin
ô	order	ᴛʜ	then
		zh	measure

ə = {
  a in about
  e in taken
  i in pencil
  o in lemon
  u in circus
}

folklore—Rip Van Winkle is famous in American **folklore.**

laugh ing stock (laf′ing stok′), person or thing that is made fun of. *n.*

leg a cy (leg′ə sē), **1** money or other property left to a person by the will of someone who has died. **2** something that has been handed down from an ancestor or predecessor. *n., pl.* **leg a cies.**

loi ter (loi′tər), **1** linger idly; stop and play along the way: *She loitered along the street, looking into all the store windows.* **2** spend (time) idly: *loiter the hours away. v.*

mis er y (miz′ər ē), an unhappy state of mind: *Think of the misery of having no home or friends. n., pl.* **mis er ies.**

mys ti fy (mis′tə fī), bewilder or confuse purposely; puzzle; perplex: *The magician's tricks mystified the audience. v.,* **mys ti fied, mys ti fy ing.**

o ver see (ō′vər sē′), look after and direct (work or workers); supervise; manage: *oversee a factory. v.,* **o ver saw, o ver seen** (ō′vər sēn′), **o ver see ing.**

o ver se er (ō′vər sē′ər), person who oversees others or their work. *n.*

parchment—The Declaration of Independence is written on **parchment.**

parch ment (pärch′mənt), **1** the skin of sheep or goats, prepared for use as a writing material. **2** manuscript or document written on parchment. **3** paper that looks like parchment. *n.*

ras cal (ras′kəl), **1** a bad, dishonest person. **2** a mischievous person. *n.*

realm (relm), **1** kingdom. **2** region; range; extent: *This is beyond the realm of my understanding.* **3** a particular field of something: *the realm of biology, the realm of poetry. n.*

sage (sāj), **1** showing wisdom or good judgment: *a sage reply.* **2** wise: *The queen surrounded herself with sage advisers.* **3** a very wise man: *The sage gave advice to his king.* **1,2** *adj.,* **sag er, sag est; 3** *n.*

sap (sap), **1** liquid that circulates through a plant, carrying water, food, etc., as blood does in animals. Rising sap carries water and minerals from the roots; sap traveling downward carries sugar, gums, resins, etc. **2** SLANG. a fool. *n.*

sap (def. 1)—**sap** being collected from a maple tree

sar casm (sär′kaz′əm), **1** a sneering or cutting remark; ironical taunt. **2** act of making fun of people to hurt their feelings; harsh or bitter irony: *"How unselfish you are!" said the little girl in sarcasm as her sister took the biggest piece of cake. n.* [*Sarcasm* comes from Greek *sarkazein*, meaning "to sneer, to strip off flesh."]

sar cas tic (sär kas′tik), using sarcasm; sneering; cutting: *"Don't hurry!" was my brother's sarcastic comment as I slowly dressed. adj.* —**sar cas′ti cal ly,** *adv.*

scorn (skôrn), look down upon; think of as mean or low; despise: *Most people scorn tattletales. v.*

seer (sir), person who foresees or foretells future events; prophet. *n.*

seize (sēz), **1** take hold of suddenly; clutch; grasp: *In fright I seized her arm.* **2** take prisoner; arrest; catch: *seize someone wanted for murder. v.,* **seized, seiz ing.**

shed¹ (shed), a building used for shelter, storage, etc., usually having only one story: *a wagon shed, a train shed. n.*

shed² (shed), **1** pour out; let flow: *shed tears.* **2** cast off; let drop or fall: *The snake sheds its skin. The umbrella sheds water.* **3** get rid of: *shed one's worries, shed one's fears. v.,* **shed, shed ding.**
shed blood, destroy life; kill.

sum mon (sum′ən), **1** to call with authority; order to come; send for: *I was summoned to the principal's office. An urgent phone call summoned me home.* **2** to call together: *summon an assembly. v.*

swin dle (swin′dl), **1** cheat; defraud: *Honest storekeepers do not swindle their customers.* **2** get by fraud. **3** a cheating act; fraud. *1,2 v.,* **swin dled, swin dling;** *3 n.*

tend en cy (ten′dən sē), likelihood; leaning: *a tendency to fight. Wood has a tendency to swell if it gets wet. n., pl.* **tend en cies.**

ver i fy (ver′ə fī), **1** prove to be true; confirm: *The driver's report of the accident was verified by two witnesses.* **2** test the correctness of; check for accuracy: *You can verify the spelling of a word by looking in a dictionary. v.,* **ver i fied, ver i fy ing.**

a hat	**oi** oil
ā age	**ou** out
ä far	**u** cup
e let	**ù** put
ē equal	**ü** rule
ėr term	
i it	**ch** child
ī ice	**ng** long
o hot	**sh** she
ō open	**th** thin
ô order	**ᴛʜ** then
	zh measure

ə = {
a in about
e in taken
i in pencil
o in lemon
u in circus
}

Acknowledgments

Text
Page 6: From *Theo Zephyr* by Dean Hughes, pages 3-22. Copyright © 1987 by Dean Hughes. Reprinted with the permission of Atheneum Books for Young Readers, an imprint of Simon & Schuster. Page 33: "The People Could Fly" from *The People Could Fly* by Virginia Hamilton. Text copyright © 1985 by Virginia Hamilton. Reprinted by permission of Alfred A. Knopf, Inc.
Page 40: "The People Could Fly: The Evolution of a Tale" by Virginia Hamilton. Copyright © 1991 by Virginia Hamilton.
Page 44: "Words Free as Confetti" by Pat Mora. Copyright © 1991 by Pat Mora.
Page 46: "Fall Leaves and Poems" by Pat Mora. Copyright © 1991 by Pat Mora.
Pages 50–55: "Grasshoppers" and "Fireflies" and illustrations from *Joyful Noise* by Paul Fleischman, illustrated by Eric Beddows. Text copyright © 1988 by Paul Fleischman. Illustrations copyright © 1988 by Eric Beddows. Reprinted by permission of HarperCollins *Publishers*.
Page 56: "Making a Joyful Noise" by Paul Fleischman. Copyright © 1991 by Paul Fleischman.
Page 60: "The Cat and the Golden Egg" from *The Town Cats and Other Tales* by Lloyd Alexander. Text copyright © 1979 by Lloyd Alexander. Used by permission of Dutton Children's Books, a division of Penguin Books USA Inc.
Page 74: "Fun + Fancy = Fantasy" by Lloyd Alexander. Copyright © 1991 by Lloyd Alexander.
Page 78: "The Rascal Crow" from *The Foundling and Other Tales of Prydain* by Lloyd Alexander. Copyright © 1973 by Lloyd Alexander. Reprinted by permission of Henry Holt and Company, Inc.
Page 93: "Cinderella Finds Time" from *Skits and Spoofs for Young Actors* by Val R. Cheatham. Copyright © 1977 by Val R. Cheatham. Reprinted by permission of Plays, Inc.
Page 108: "In Search of Cinderella" from *A Light in the Attic* by Shel Silverstein. Copyright © 1981 by Evel Eye Music, Inc. Reprinted by permission of HarperCollins *Publishers*.
Page 109: "Glass Slipper" by Jane Yolen. Copyright © 1992 by Jane Yolen.

Page 110: "... And Then the Prince Knelt Down and Tried to Put the Glass Slipper on Cinderella's Foot" from *If I Were in Charge of the World and Other Worries* by Judith Viorst, page 29. Copyright © 1981 by Judith Viorst. Reprinted with the permission of Atheneum Books for Young Readers, an imprint of Simon & Schuster.
Page 112: *Yeh-Shen, A Cinderella Story from China*, retold by Ai-Ling Louie, illustrated by Ed Young. Text copyright © 1982 by Ai-Ling Louie, illustrations copyright © 1982 by Ed Young. Reprinted by permission of Philomel Books.

Artists
Illustrations owned and copyrighted by the illustrator.
Cover: Lisa Desimini
Pages 1–4: Lisa Desimini
Pages 7–31: Jeff Meyer
Pages 32–43: Leo and Diane Dillon
Pages 44–49: Lois Ehlert
Pages 50–59: Eric Beddows
Pages 60–91, 127: Kinuko Craft
Pages 92–93: Richard Kehl
Page 108: Shel Silverstein
Pages 110-111: Ryle Smith
Pages 112–126: Ed Young

Photographs
Page 40: Courtesy of Virginia Hamilton
Page 46: Courtesy of Pat Mora
Page 56: Courtesy of Paul Fleischman
Page 74: Courtesy of Lloyd Alexander
Page 132: The Granger Collection, New York
Page 134 bottom: Fred Whitehead/Earth Scenes
Unless otherwise acknowledged, all photographs are the property of ScottForesman.

Glossary
The contents of the Glossary entries in this book have been adapted from *Scott, Foresman Intermediate Dictionary*, Copyright © 1988 by Scott, Foresman and Company, and *Scott, Foresman Advanced Dictionary*, Copyright © 1988 by Scott, Foresman and Company.